And will your Ladyship ever remain cruel, & insensible to emotions which you alone can excite? —

Oh you flatterer! Every body knows your devotion for *Woods* & *Forests*: therefor don't talk to me of Love, false man! my heart bleeds only for my persecuted friends of the true Church in Ireland. You are the only man in christendom who is able to emancipate them. Grant me this favor dearest, most illustrious hero and then — *perhaps* — I could — —

WELLINGTON AND THE ARBUTHNOTS

Harriet Arbuthnot, painted in 1816 by Sir Thomas Lawrence

WELLINGTON AND THE ARBUTHNOTS

A TRIANGULAR FRIENDSHIP

E.A. SMITH

ALAN SUTTON PUBLISHING LIMITED

First published in the United Kingdom in 1994
Alan Sutton Publishing Limited · Phoenix Mill · Far Thrupp · Stroud
Gloucestershire

First published in the United States of America in 1994
Alan Sutton Publishing Inc. · 83 Washington Street · Dover · NH 03820

British Library Cataloguing in Publication Data

Smith, E.A.
 Wellington and the Arbuthnots: Triangular Friendship
 I. Title
 941.07092

ISBN 0–7509–0629–4

Library of Congress Cataloging in Publication Data applied for

Jacket illustrations: front: The Duke of Wellington, *by Sir Thomas
Lawrence (Victoria & Albert Museum),* Harriet Arbuthnot, *by Sir
Thomas Lawrence (private collection); back: detail from* Morning . . .
Night, *by W. Heath ('Paul Pry') (author's collection).*

Typeset in 12/13 Times.
Typesetting and origination by
Alan Sutton Publishing Limited.
Printed in Great Britain by
Hartnolls Ltd, Bodmin, Cornwall.

Contents

For Virginia
with love

List of Illustrations

Illustrations are reproduced by kind permission of the following: *Frontispiece*: private collection. No.1, Country Life Picture Library; Nos 2, 7, 16, Mrs M. Fry; No. 6, The National Maritime Museum; Nos 10, 13, 14, 15, 36, The National Portrait Gallery; Nos 11, 37, The Victoria and Albert Museum; No.12, The Duke of Wellington; No. 17, Royal Pavilion, Art Gallery and Museums, Brighton; No. 20, The Principal, Fellows and Scholars of Jesus College, Oxford; Nos 8, 22, 28, 30–35, the University of Reading; Nos 5, 9, 18, 19, 21, 23, 24, 29, 38, are from the author's collection.

Photography: Cover (Harriet Arbuthnot) and frontispiece by Helen Pugh-Cook; No. 1 by *Country Life*; Nos 2, 7, and 16 by Roger Mockford; Nos 3, 4, 5, 8, 9, 18, 19, 21–35 by Reading University Library; No. 12 by the Courtauld Institute.

Preface

The relationship between the Duke of Wellington and Harriet Arbuthnot was one of the most prominent, and notorious, friendships in English society in the early nineteenth century. The duke's marriage, it was well known, was an unsuccessful one and although there was no formal separation or attempt at divorce he and his wife had nothing in common and spent little time together. Wellington sought other female companions to fill the gap in his life. Prominent among those women friends was Harriet, wife of Charles Arbuthnot, who was an active political figure in the second rank of Lord Liverpool's government. She was born Harriet Fane, a member of an aristocratic but impoverished family closely related to the earls of Westmorland, and she was twenty-six years younger than her husband, whose first wife had died in 1806, eight years before he married Harriet. These circumstances gave rise to suspicions that the duke's relations with Harriet were more than merely friendly. He spent a good deal of time with her in London during the parliamentary season and in the country, at the Arbuthnots' home in Northamptonshire, at his own residence at Stratfield Saye in Hampshire, and at country house parties during the rest of the year.

Harriet was fascinated by politics and eager to know the secrets of government and to influence men in power. She was at first an admirer of Lord Castlereagh, Liverpool's Foreign Secretary, whom she had known since her youth. After Castlereagh's tragic death in 1822 she transferred her affections to Wellington whom she had met in Paris in 1815. For the rest of her life she was the duke's closest confidante and she made no secret of her admiration for his achievements and his political principles, which she shared as a lifelong Tory.

Nevertheless, as this book maintains, the relationship between Harriet and Wellington was not a sexual one, and, far from its being clandestine, they frequently appeared in public together and her husband Charles played an equal role in it. The evidence shows beyond doubt that Harriet was a loving and faithful wife whose devotion was to her husband and to no other man. Together, the Arbuthnots provided what was lacking in Wellington's life, a quiet domestic atmosphere in which the duke could talk freely about political affairs without fear that his conversation would be disclosed to anyone else, and where he could listen to advice, which was not tinged with flattery, but sometimes contrary to his own views. Charles's experience as a long-serving politician who was privy to the closest secrets of government was as invaluable to Wellington as was Harriet's sympathetic but critical ear. The three formed what Elizabeth Longford, in her biography of the duke, has termed 'a most unusual, subtle, and successful essay in triangular friendship.'

This book traces the origins and course of that friendship from the beginning to the end of the lives of the three participants. Its nature as an equilateral triangle is shown by the circumstance that, after the deaths of their two wives, Charles and the duke lived harmoniously together until Charles's death in 1850, only two years before that of the duke. In many ways it was Charles rather than Harriet who stood at the centre of the relationship, and his career is here fully examined and evaluated for the first time. His importance is borne out by the fact that he was valued as a friend by no less than King George IV, with whom he cooperated in promoting that artistic monarch's plans to make London a worthy capital for a great Empire.

I am grateful to all those who have helped me to tell this story. My particular thanks are due to Mrs Mary Fry and Mr Julian Fane for their kind hospitality at Fulbeck, and for permission to use the family papers. I am also grateful to the owner of the original portrait of Harriet by Sir Thomas Lawrence for permission to reproduce it. The engraving of the portrait of Marcia Arbuthnot is in my possession. The portraits of Charles Arbuthnot in old age and of the Duke of Wellington are reproduced by courtesy of the Victoria and Albert Museum. Other illustrations are acknowledged on p. viii.

My thanks are also due to the librarians at King's College, Aberdeen, and at the University Library, Southampton, for their assistance in my research into the Arbuthnot and the Wellington papers respectively and to the staff of the Lincolnshire County Record Office for their help in my work on the Fane papers. I am grateful to Sir William Arbuthnot, bart, for permission to use and quote from the Arbuthnot papers, and to the staff of the British Library Department of MSS for access to the papers in their care listed in the bibliography.

I am also grateful to the Macmillan Press Ltd for permission to quote from *The Journal of Mrs Arbuthnot 1820–1832*, ed. F. Bamford and the Duke of Wellington (1950).

Special thanks are due as always to Mrs E. Berry for reducing my MS to readable typescript and to my editor, Anne Bennett, for her efficient work on the book. My debt to Virginia, my wife, is immeasurable. She has taken a close interest in this book from its beginnings and I have profited more than I can say from her help and criticism. I dedicate it to her as a small token of my gratitude.

1 Harriet Fane

Fulbeck was, and still is, one of the most attractive villages in Lincolnshire. Sited off the main road from Lincoln to Grantham, it lies between the fens to the east and the plain of Newark to the west in a fold of the hills which form the spine of this flat county. Its steep main street runs down from the Hall and medieval church with its high, pinnacled tower, now much Victorianized, past a small green into the valley of the beck which gives the village its name. Along the main street and back round to the church lie houses and farms of yellow stone with orange-coloured clay tile roofs. At the end of the eighteenth century the church, though much dilapidated, served a community of some four hundred souls scattered over the 3,900 acres of the parish. Their more material needs were served by two public houses, the Hare and Hounds and the Six Bells, and on less happy occasions by the stocks and pillory which still stood beside the broken shaft of the village cross by the churchyard. It was a quiet, peaceful place, a typical country village where the open fields were still portioned out in strips on the medieval plan until the enclosure and consolidation of the farms in 1805. This backwardness meant that the deferential tenants and labouring people accepted with little question, at least outside the alehouses, the superior status and economic power of the owners of the Hall and their relatives in the nearby manor house, and the moral authority of the resident clergyman, inevitably a younger son from the Hall.

In the last decade of the eighteenth century the Hall was occupied by members of the Fane family, as it had been since the early seventeenth century and still is today. The Fanes were supposed to be of Welsh origin but the real founder of the family was Henry Vane, a yeoman of Tonbridge in Kent at the end of the fifteenth century. Despite his humble origins he was destined to be the ancestor of the Vanes, Dukes of Cleveland, of Barnard Castle in County Durham, and the Fanes who became Earls of Westmorland, Lords le Despenser and Burghersh. Henry's third son Thomas prospered in the City of London, while his second son Henry married the widow of a Surrey squire and also fathered a bastard son Ralph who was a henchman of Thomas Cromwell in Henry VIII's time and then of Protector Somerset under

Edward VI. He failed to escape the common fate of such partisans in that insecure age and was hanged on Tower Hill in 1552. The elder line of Henry senior's descendants ran from his eldest son John, through *his* son Richard, described as a gentleman of Tudeley in Kent, and in the next generation through George, High Sheriff of Kent under Mary I. The family's somewhat stormy history was maintained when George's elder son, Sir Thomas Fane, was implicated in Wyatt's rebellion against Mary I, but he survived, was pardoned, and advanced the family fortunes by taking as his second wife Mary, a daughter of Lord Abergavenny and member of the powerful northern family of Neville of Raby and owners of Mereworth Castle in Kent. Their son Francis inherited from his mother the barony of le Despenser and as a favourite of James I was advanced to the barony of Burghersh and earldom of Westmorland. His wife was also well connected, being the daughter of Sir Anthony Mildmay of Apethorpe, Northants., which became one of the family seats of the later Earls of Westmorland, and granddaughter of Sir Walter Mildmay, the redoubtable Puritan leader of Elizabeth's time and founder of Emmanuel College, Cambridge, where several of his descendants were to study.

The seventeenth century was hardly less turbulent, and dangerous to the upper classes, than the sixteenth and the Fanes were inevitably embroiled in the civil wars between Charles I and Parliament. Mildmay Fane, the second earl, went over to Parliament from the King in 1643 while his younger brother, Sir Francis Fane, who had acquired Fulbeck Hall, remained a courtier and commanded the King's forces at Doncaster and Lincoln. He too proved to be a survivor. He was allowed by the Republic to buy back his confiscated estate, and before the Restoration of Charles II in 1660 occupied his time in rebuilding the Hall in Restoration style and in travelling 'into Holland, Denmark, Germany, Loraigne, Switzerland, Italy, Naples, France and Flanders' with a faithful servant of fifty years named Thomas Ball, whose monument in the church so described their travels and their conclusion 'with ye Preacher, there was nothing new under the sun and y^t all was Vanity and only one thing necessary, to fear God and keep his commandments'. His son, also Sir Francis, maintained his father's royalist sympathies and became a figure at the court of Charles II, where he wrote plays and poems, one of which, entitled 'Love in the Dark', he dedicated to Rochester, the king's dissolute favourite.

After the second Sir Francis the Fanes seem to have retreated from court life, though their cousin the 5th Earl of Westmorland was a favourite of William III after the Glorious Revolution. The family also ran out of heirs. Sir Francis's son had only one male descendant, who died childless. His widow inherited Fulbeck and passed it on her death in 1767 to another Henry Fane, a second cousin once removed. The senior branch of the family ran into similar troubles, and on the death of the 7th Earl of Westmorland without direct heirs in 1762 the earldom and estates passed to a descendant of Thomas Fane, a Bristol attorney. Fulbeck Hall also passed to the new Earl of Westmorland who rented it out between 1762 and 1783, when he gave it to his younger son, Henry, who settled there with his wife and growing family.

This Henry Fane, forced as a younger son to earn his living, had been a clerk in the Treasury but was described in a report to the Earl of Bute at the beginning of George III's reign as 'very idle and careless of his duty and spending much time in the country'. He was more concerned with his family's financial business 'to the injury of his seniors in the [Treasury] office'. In 1772 he was shunted off into the profitable sinecure office of Keeper of the King's Private Roads, Gates, and Bridges (etc.), and during this period he fathered an illegitimate son named Henry Chamberlain, who was later to be British Consul at Lisbon and at Rio de Janeiro, and was made a baronet in 1828. He followed and accompanied a long list of Fanes as eighteenth- and early nineteenth-century Members of Parliament for Lyme Regis, a borough under the control of the Earls of Westmorland. They were all quiet backbench Tory gentlemen: not one of the nine between 1757 and 1826 seems to have uttered a word in the House of Commons and they were steady supporters of every government of the period except on the rare occasions when the Whigs got into office. Henry sat as one of the two members for the borough from 1772 to 1802; his eldest son Henry inherited the seat from 1802 to 1818 and Vere, the fourth son, held it from 1818 to 1826. All kept silence, and all attended irregularly – the second Henry particularly so as he was serving abroad in the army most of the time.

In 1777 Henry Fane married at the age of thirty-nine. His bride, twenty years his junior, was Anne Batson, daughter of Edward Buckley Batson, a partner in a London banking house in Lombard Street and possessor of a small estate near Ringwood, Hants., and one at Upwood, Dorset, between Blandford and Shaftesbury, where he built an 'elegant' house. These properties were to be inherited by Anne in 1810, much to the relief of the Fane family's straitened finances. Those finances were strained by the expense of a large family – Anne had fourteen children in the first eighteen years of her marriage – and by the consequent need to enlarge and refurnish Fulbeck Hall which they occupied in 1784.

The house at Fulbeck had passed through several vicissitudes since the seventeenth century. Remodelled before the Restoration by Sir Francis Fane, it was burnt down on 30 December 1731 in a fire which 'consumed the Hall and all or much the greatest part of the furniture

Fulbeck Hall, sketched in 1805 by J.C. Nattes

and other goods and chattels of Francis Fane therein to his very great loss and inconvenience'. It was rebuilt in basically its present form between 1732 and 1733 by Francis Fane IV. The architect is unknown, but was probably a local man from Stamford, for it bears a strong stylistic resemblance to the town's architecture of this period. Its style is a provincial blend of English baroque, with touches of the fashionable Palladian beloved of the English aristocracy and landed gentry of the early Hanoverian period. 'Palladianism' was closely associated with Whig politics through the patronage of the dominant Whig aristocracy of the time, while Toryism remained, in reaction, devoted to the older 'native' style of Wren, Vanburgh and Hawkesmoor. As a Tory family, the Fanes were not inclined to follow too slavishly the 'modern' Whig fashion and the Hall consequently did not receive the full Palladian treatment. The new building consisted of a rectangular three-storey block with a façade of five bays divided by giant doric pilasters, set in a compact park beside the main Grantham road and approached through elaborate wrought-iron gates made in 1733 and still in use. In 1784 Henry Fane added a new north wing of two storeys containing a dining-room with a fine Adam mantelpiece and decorations, with two bedrooms and dressing-rooms above. Further additions and alterations were made after his death in 1802, financed by his widow's inheritance from her father in 1810. She added a third storey over the dining-room wing and a new entrance porch and flanking bay windows at the front, bringing the house into more or less its present state.

Fulbeck formed a comfortable, quiet, elegant and yet unpretentious home for a close-knit and affectionate family. A seventeenth-century Earl of Westmorland had celebrated the house in verse, concluding:

I'll say no more, but judg all these comprize
And christen Fulbeck Earthly Paradise.

Henry and Anne's nine sons and five daughters, of whom three died in infancy, must have agreed with their ancestor's view. In many ways they were typical of that middling but well-connected country gentry so familiar to modern readers in the novels of Jane Austen. Their social status was unquestioned, they moved in county society at the upper levels and they had access to the opportunities for careers and marriages reserved for gentlemen and young ladies of respectable family. Their close relationship to their Westmorland cousins was sustained by frequent visits to Apethorpe in neighbouring Northamptonshire, and they visited London every year when the children were growing up for Anne to introduce her girls into society. The boys went to 'good' public schools – three to Eton, three to Charterhouse – and though the younger sons who could not expect provision from the family estates had to find careers to support themselves, they all succeeded in their chosen professions, three in the army, and one each in the navy, the law, the Church, the Bengal Civil Service, and banking, the last, Vere Fane, taking up the connections of his mother's family and of one of his brothers-in-law to become a partner in Praed's bank in Fleet Street.

The sons in the army were led by Henry, the eldest, who was entered in the 4th Dragoon Guards in 1792 at the age of thirteen while still at Eton, was a Lieutenant-Colonel at nineteen, and at sixteen became ADC to his cousin the 10th Earl of Westmorland who had gone to Ireland as Lord Lieutenant in 1790. In Dublin he fell in love with the wife of Edward Cooke, a prominent Irish politician, and although Cooke eventually agreed to a separation the couple did not live together as man and wife until 1801. They had six children. Henry then moved on to serve in the campaigns against France, commanded a Portuguese cavalry division in the Peninsula under Wellington, and distinguished himself in peacetime, eventually becoming Commander-in-Chief in India in 1835. His father, who died in 1802, never knew of his son's connection with Mrs Cooke, and she and her children were never recognized by Henry's mother. Henry's family lived near Ringwood, where his companion was known as 'Lady Fane'. Their eldest son, also Henry, went to India on his father's staff, became a Lieutenant-Colonel, and owned Fulbeck from 1840 to 1882. Their second son Vere was lost at sea in 1826, aged nineteen, and the third son Arthur who was born in 1810 took Holy Orders, and became Vicar of Warminster where his widowed mother lived with him. He succeeded his uncle Edward as Rector of Fulbeck.

The second of Anne's sons, Charles, followed his brother to Eton and into the army. He served in the Coldstream Guards in Egypt in 1801 and then in Spain. Wounded in the retreat to Corunna in 1809, he recovered to fight at Vittoria four years later, where he died of wounds received from a cannon shot in leading his regiment in a charge against the French. The third son, Vere, who became the banker, was the one Anne relied on to manage the family's financial affairs after her husband's death, and Edward, who entered the Church and became Rector of Fulbeck, looked after estate business as well as attending to his pastoral duties. Nevile, who entered the navy, was another to die young, being drowned at Barbados in 1808, aged twenty-six. William went to India in the East India Company's Civil Service in 1808, married in 1811 and had eight children. He died on leave in Cape Town in 1839. Mildmay, the seventh son, followed his elder brothers into the army, served in the Peninsula, fought and was wounded at Quatre Bras before Waterloo in 1815, and followed his brothers to India as a Lieutenant-Colonel in 1829. He returned to live at Fulbeck after his retirement and was killed in a fall when hunting in 1869. Finally, Robert George Cecil, the youngest son, educated at Charterhouse and Magdalen, Oxford, went into law and was appointed a Commissioner in Bankruptcy. His sister Harriet, writing to Robert Peel in 1826 to try to secure him an appointment as a Commissioner for enquiry into charities, pointed out that he took a first-class degree at Oxford and was *'really very clever'*.

As the sons, except for Vere and Edward, left Fulbeck to go to school or to serve in their professions, the daughters were left much to their own society. One, Elizabeth, died shortly before her father in 1802 at the age of nineteen. The other three sisters were Anne, Caroline, and Harriet. Anne, the eldest daughter and the second of the children, was born on 19 January 1780 and in 1803 she married General John Michel of Dulish, Dorset. Caroline, the second surviving daughter, was born on 28 December 1791 and Harriet on 10 September 1793. They were the closest of the sisters. They were sent to school in their teens but also educated at home, as was the custom of the time, under a French governess, Mlle Françix, whom Harriet described in 1826 as 'an excellent old woman' whom she had known for over twenty years. The sisters acquired the necessary accomplishments of fashionable young ladies. Sketching, needlework, music and reading, aloud to their mother or to themselves, occupied their indoor hours, and they took daily exercise riding or walking through the fields and byways around the village. They also enjoyed amateur dramatics and performed Shakespearean plays with their

The Fane sisters, Anne, Harriet and Caroline in Much Ado about Nothing. *Watercolour by Thomas Heaphy*

family. Thomas Heaphy produced in 1810 a colour sketch of the three sisters, Anne, Caroline, and Harriet, in the roles of Hero, Beatrice, and Ursula in a scene from *Much Ado about Nothing*.

The sisters were not always by themselves but enjoyed a close relationship with their brothers. Harriet was especially fond of Charles, the second brother and twelve years her senior. His tragic death in battle in 1813, at the time of her difficulties over her engagement to Charles Arbuthnot, affected her deeply. 'I have done nothing all day', she wrote, 'but wander about alone in the walks we used to frequent together and utter unavailing cries of agony and despair at the conviction that these days of happiness are fled for ever.' Harriet was also, as the youngest daughter, especially close to her mother to whom convention as well as affection dictated that she should be a companion. Caroline, three years older, was the first to marry in 1812, when she became the wife of Charles Chaplin, a Lincolnshire squire and Member of Parliament. Harriet meanwhile had fallen in love with her future husband whom she was to marry early in 1814.

The Battle of Vittoria, 21 June 1813. Drawing by W. Heath from Wellington Victories *(c. 1815)*

If the quiet domesticity of the family mirrored the portrait of county society painted by Jane Austen, it could hardly be the case that their lives were unaffected, as is sometimes claimed of Jane Austen's characters, by the long wars raging against Revolutionary and Napoleonic France. Three brothers away on active service in the army, of whom one was killed and two wounded, and one drowned while on naval service, brought home the destructive effects of the wars which broke out in the year of Harriet's birth and which ended only eighteen months after her marriage. She lived all her girlhood in a country whose economic resources and manpower were stretched by a war more far-reaching in its effects than any previous war in its history. Taxation, though hardly severe by modern wartime standards, was unprecedentedly high, there were occasional food shortages due to bad harvests, especially in the 1790s, and it was not only the landed gentry whose sons, and fathers, had to go away to war, leaving their families to fend for themselves. The Hall was not shut off from the village by high walls but lay close to and was an integral part of it. It was natural that Harriet and her sisters would have played the part expected of the upper classes in that period in visiting and helping to support the wives and families of ordinary men from the village who had to serve in the regular forces or the county militia. At the same time the parades and displays of the Yeomanry and Volunteer corps who were recruited to preserve internal order and to relieve the regular army of internal police duties kept the sounds and sights of military life much in the forefront of their lives. Growing up in England at that time even in the relatively comfortable world of the gentry and aristocracy did not insulate young men and women from the realities of war and deprivation. Above all, continental travel was almost impossible, certainly for adolescent girls. It was not until after her marriage and the defeat of Napoleon that Harriet was able to persuade her husband to take her for the first time to Paris. Until then, her overseas experience was limited to Ireland, where the family had friends and connections, and where she fell in love for the first time.

Harriet was the most beautiful of the Fane sisters, and she remained an attractive woman throughout her life. She was lively, intelligent, and had strong opinions. She grew up in a strongly Tory household and absorbed and reflected those views in her personal and political life. She was a woman of strong moral principles and deep Christian convictions. She condemned Lord Byron, she wrote in 1824, 'highly gifted as he was and perverting the talents which Nature gave him by his diabolical efforts to turn into ridicule every moral and religious feeling, far, far worse than a thief or robber who may plead ignorance or want as an excuse'. His writings were 'so profligate they are not fit to be read'. The Duke of Wellington who became a close friend remarked after her death that 'there was nothing brilliant about her, but that she was a woman of strong sense, with a mind that turned to matters of fact, and very inquisitive about them.' She was, wrote one of the duke's biographers, 'a deeply conventional and faithful wife' whose 'special gift lay in devoting herself exclusively to whatever subject occupied her at the moment – her estate and garden, her stepchildren, society, politics.' Harriet was passionately interested in political affairs, and her friendships with Castlereagh and later Wellington were founded on her admiration for their political principles and unswerving consistency rather than on physical attraction. Though attractive both in appearance and in character, after her marriage she never looked at any man but her husband; though the world sometimes gossiped about her relationship with Wellington, the most cursory reading of her journal and correspondence makes it clear that she was never interested in any other man for any reason but politics. Her strictures on women like Lady Strachan or Mrs Fox, who had low moral reputations and had affairs with other men, show a genuine disgust for immoral behaviour of any kind. She was, in truth, neither romantic in disposition nor particularly imaginative, nor was she much concerned about others' opinions. Her feet were firmly on the ground, and Wellington valued her not only for the domestic companionship he lacked in his own home but for her strength of character and as a staunch supporter and reliable adviser in his political life. One of Wellington's friends remarked in later years that when he first met her in 1828:

she was still most attractive. The bloom of youth might indeed be gone, but there remained the soft brown eye, a profusion of brown silky hair, features both regular and expressive, and a figure singularly graceful. But there was much more to admire in her than this. To great natural abilities there was added a large stock of knowledge, acquired both from books and from intercourse with men. Her conversation was in consequence always agreeable, often brilliant, without the slightest apparent effort made to go out of the common ruck. To her likewise belonged a charm, which, when intellectual women can boast of it, renders them mistresses of all hearts.

This was the mature Harriet, tempered by experience of the world, fascinated by politics, and still as much in love with her husband as when they became engaged. He was not her first love: they met in 1807 when she was still a schoolgirl of fourteen, but as he was forty, the father of four young children and recently widowed, no more than polite conversation passed between them. In any case Harriet soon afterwards fell in love with Thomas Capel, youngest son of the Earl of Essex, and a Captain in the Royal Navy, who had fought at Trafalgar and who was eventually to become an Admiral. Her feelings, however, do not seem to have been reciprocated, and she later told her husband that shortly afterwards when she met Lord Castlereagh on a visit to Ireland he, not knowing of her feelings for Capel, asked her whether it was true that he was going to marry Lady Georgiana Cecil: 'Had he looked at me he would have seen what I felt', Harriet wrote, 'but he did not observe the effect of his question, and went on talking on some other subject.' Capel in fact married someone else, and Harriet's affections remained unengaged until the winter of 1812–13 when she and her future husband met for the third time and fell in love. The course of that love was not to be smooth, for several reasons, some of them deriving from the character and position of the man she was to marry.

2 'Gosh'

Charles Arbuthnot's background was very different from the conventional upper-class upbringing of his second wife. His family were impoverished Scots gentry from Aberdeenshire and his father, named John, had to make his own way in the world, which he did with considerable eccentricity and variable success. He sold his property in Scotland in 1760, seven years before Charles was born, and set up house at Ravensbury near Mitcham in Surrey where he carried out experiments in agriculture, particularly in the cultivation of madder. He became a correspondent and close friend of Arthur Young, the agricultural journalist and pioneer, who wrote that he found him 'the most agreeable, pleasant and interesting connection which I ever made in agricultural pursuits'. When the Empress Catherine of Russia sent over seven or eight young men to learn practical agriculture in England, two or three were sent to John Arbuthnot. He also wrote pamphlets on the cultivation of grasses and on the enclosure of commons and waste lands to increase food production to feed the rapidly growing population, but his own experiments were not successful. In 1781 he was obliged to give up his farm to his relation Admiral John Marriott Arbuthnot who foreclosed on a mortgage of £5,000 which Arbuthnot failed to repay. In the following year his third wife Anne, daughter of Richard Stone, a London banker, of Lombard Street, and Charles's mother, died. The Scots politician and lawyer Lord Loughborough rescued him from ruin by securing him a post as an Inspector-General for the Irish Linen Board at a salary of £500 p.a. He went to live in Ireland, first in Dublin, and from 1786 on an estate in County Mayo where he began to build a country house. Not uncharacteristically, it was still unfinished at his death in 1797.

John Arbuthnot married five times and had a total of eleven children, of whom Charles was the third, being the second by his third wife. He left all his property to his younger children, the rest, he wrote, 'being sufficiently provided for' already. In Charles's case that provision came from his mother's relations, to whom he was sent when quite young by parents who, a descendant wrote, 'were, perhaps, only too thankful – with their large family and fluctuating fortunes – to transfer the burden of his education and launching on a career' to others. Fortunately those relations were well connected. One great-uncle, George Stone, was Primate of Ireland, the other was Andrew Stone who was Under-Secretary of State in the Duke of Newcastle's government in 1734, became Newcastle's confidant and 'man of business', private secretary to King George II in 1748, and from 1751 a tutor to the Prince of Wales, later George III. Charles's later career in politics might almost have been modelled on that of his great-uncle. Both served 'behind the scenes' as the men who oiled the wheels and got things done for their more prominent masters, and by their hard work and dedication to the details of patronage and financial business kept the political machine running.

Charles was born on 14 March 1767 at Ravensbury. He seems to have been neglected by his parents, and developed little affection for them in return. He was much fonder of his great-uncle Andrew and when, quite early in his childhood, he was sent to visit him, as he later recalled, when the carriage came to take him back he burst into tears and his uncle 'seeing me so unhappy at the thought of going away' resolved to let him stay. He settled happily into the Stones' household, but Andrew Stone died when Charles was seven, and he was then sent to a private school at Richmond and five years later to Westminster. He continued to live with his great-aunt in the holidays and after her death with her unmarried sister and his aunt Mrs Sarah Stone. His great-uncle left him £3,000 and settled on him a further £20,000, to be received after the deaths of his great-aunt and her sister. He not only had nothing from his parents but, after his father's business failure in 1781 when he was fourteen, he never saw his mother again – she went to live abroad and died a year later – and saw his father only on his very occasional visits to England. He later declared that 'His parents were little more than names to him'. His brothers and sisters too were strangers until they grew up and returned from Ireland. His mother's relations were the only family he really knew or cared for.

In 1784 at the age of seventeen Charles arrived at Christ Church, Oxford and proceeded to spend his fortune. He wrote in a fragmentary autobiography intended for his children that at Westminster he had been 'a pretty good scholar' but at Oxford 'I passed my whole time in idleness and amusements' with 'a most agreeable set' of companions, who no doubt helped him to spend his money. Among these friends was George Canning, who wrote in 1794 that, though they had never been intimate friends, 'I am very fond of him, and like of all things to meet him. . . . He is pleasant, quick, gentlemanly and universally a favourite.' Charles was popular and highly sociable. He acquired the nickname 'Gosh', which stuck to him all his life among his friends. He wrote to another friend John Sneyd on one occasion that even 'my common acquaintance call me Gosh! I am afraid I am too good-natured, which is the reason why I don't awe people. I like a few to call me so, but I reckon it is a privilege that ought to be kept rather sacred. Many people believe that my name is Mr Gosh. Some lady at the opera asked [Charles] Greville my name. "It is Mr Gosh." "Dear! what an odd name!"'

Charles was also fond of female company, not always of the most respectable kind. He once asked Sneyd to see and report on a child born to one Miss, or Mrs Goodman whom he found it necessary to recognize as his son, 'naively confessing that his wish that it was so was possibly the father to the thought'. As he thought the boy would not wish to be known by his mother's name he suggested he should be called 'Gosh'. He had other love affairs, at least one of which was serious enough to cause him to write 'pages of heartbroken lamentation' to Sneyd after the lady's early death. In 1814 Lady Charlotte Bury referred to 'a person whom twenty years ago, he had been madly in love with' meeting him again with his second wife at a party. His affections were evidently often stirred.

At Oxford or shortly afterwards he also seems to have taken up, either seriously or, more likely, in fun, a system of faith-healing known by the name of its founder, Main-a-Duc. He assured his friends that it could cure any complaint at a distance of hundreds of miles. Another friend, Lord Titchfield, told Sneyd that 'Arbuthnot is not in Bedlam, nor has he yet worn the strait waistcoat, but I am afraid that his attachment to Main-a-Ducism may very possibly reduce him to one of those two extremities. His plan now is to convince you of the powers and excellence of what he calls the Science by making you dog-sick at a certain hour of which he will inform you. Two of his friends join him in this good-natured combination to lighten your darkness at the expense of your health.'

After leaving Oxford Charles continued to live a life of idleness until he reached the age of twenty-five. He had at first been intended for the Bar, but, he wrote, 'the severe labour of the law' was uncongenial and he preferred to travel in Europe with two of his Oxford friends, the Duke of Dorset and a Mr Temple, his great-uncle's generosity making it unnecessary to hurry into earning a living. They spent several months in Vienna and Charles then went on to Poland in 1789. Here he moved in court circles, writing that he 'lived a great deal with Stanislaus, the last of the Kings of Poland' and that 'I became intimately acquainted with men and women of the highest talent and rank, and whose society was delightful'. There, and back in London in the early years of the 1790s he indulged his love of society, conversation and dining-out, moving among a wide circle of acquaintances. Canning recorded of a dinner at

Charles Arbuthnot as a young man, from a miniature

the Gowers' in Wimbledon in April 1794, at which Arbuthnot was present, that 'I do not recollect to have passed a more delightful evening for some time than we four . . . with books and conversation in the library.' In the previous December he and Arbuthnot had similarly dined at Lord Grenville's with Pitt, Lord Mornington, Lord Mulgrave, and Robert Banks Jenkinson and found Arbuthnot 'in great favour with Lord Grenville'.

Enjoyable as was the life of a man-about-town, with the coming of the French war in 1793 Charles confessed that 'I often had misgivings in my own mind and was dissatisfied with the idle life that I was passing'. The time had come to settle on a career. He thought at first of the army, and joined a new regiment being raised by his friend Lord Paget, the future Marquess of Anglesey and veteran of Waterloo. It was to be the 80th Regiment of Foot, or the Staffordshire Volunteers, the officers to be 'young Gentlemen, above sixteen years of age', the men over 5ft 6in. in height, 'with a good countenance, straight, and well made'. The officers' uniforms, devised by Paget, had yellow facings, gold epaulettes and gold laced hat and white feather 'with a very handsome sword' for afternoon dress, and in the mornings a jacket, blue pantaloons with yellow stripes and a bearskin helmet. It was to be a very fashionable regiment, but Charles's friends decided that a civilian career would suit him better and persuaded him to resign, perhaps showing a shrewder appreciation of where his talents might lie. One friend, John King, was Under-Secretary of State to Lord Grenville in the Foreign Office, and helped to get Charles the post of précis writer in the office at a salary of £300 a year. Canning thought it a better post than the comparable one occupied by his friend John Hookham Frere at the Home Office because the work was more interesting and the salary better. For Charles it was the start of a career in diplomacy that lasted for twelve years. He quickly impressed Lord Grenville and the Prime Minister, William Pitt, whom he already knew socially, with his talents. Canning wrote that he was 'pleasant, quick, gentlemanly and universally a favourite', while Charles himself declared that the post opened up 'a great fund of information' which would fit him for 'higher situations', while providentially saving him from 'the high road to ruin' on which he had been travelling.

However, Charles did not yet commit himself fully to a career in government office. He declared to Pitt in January 1795 that he wished to take an active part in supporting his administration in Parliament, and gained the promise of a seat in the House of Commons for a constituency controlled by government influence. In March of that year a vacancy occurred in the Cornish pocket borough of East Looe, and Charles was elected by nomination of the patron, who had placed the seat at Pitt's disposal. He had to give up his official salary, as receipt of an office of profit under government would have disqualified him from sitting in Parliament, but he thought it worthwhile to take up this new prospect for the future.

A few months after he took his seat a new opportunity arose in the diplomatic service. Henry Wellesley, a career diplomat, later Lord Cowley, youngest brother of Arthur, later Duke of Wellington, returned to England from the post of Chargé des Affaires in Stockholm and the situation was offered to Charles in exchange for his post in the Foreign Office. Charles received the appointment in May 1795, and retained his seat in Parliament only until the next general election in the following year.

Charles stayed for two years in Stockholm as Chargé des Affaires and Secretary of the Legation, an important post in view of the value of the Baltic to British economic and strategic interests in wartime, but he failed to prevent Sweden from drifting towards support of French interests rather than British. The home government's lack of support was equally to blame and Charles's efforts gained general approval from his superiors. In February 1798, some time after his return to England, he was chosen for a special mission to Stuttgart to carry the King's official congratulations to his son-in-law Frederick of Würtemburg on succeeding to the Duchy. He proved popular and agreeable to the duchess, who wrote to her father that he 'has given here the greatest satisfaction by the propriety of his conduct'. He showed his talent for diplomacy by smoothing the ruffled feathers of the duke's minister, Count Zeppelin, who conceived himself offended at not having been favoured with a personal letter from George III or from Pitt. Charles accompanied his assurances 'with expressions which I thought would be personally most flattering to him' and which he assured Grenville were immediately effective.

Grenville had now adopted Charles as a suitable recipient of his patronage, and John King, the Under-Secretary, was still working on his behalf. He needed a well-paid appointment because he had now fallen in love with Lord Cholmondeley's niece, Marcia, the daughter of William Clapcott Lisle, a country gentleman of Upway in Dorset, by Hester, sister of the first Marquess of Cholmondeley, who was now lady-in-waiting to the Princess of Wales. Charles wrote to Lord Grenville of 'a conversation with Lord Cholmondeley, who confessed to me that he saw a very great chance of my being successful [in his courtship] if I could obtain such an income as would meet with the family's approbation'.

Grenville, prompted by John King, responded generously. He assured King that he was 'desirous of doing an act of friendship' towards

Charles, and offered the choice of two diplomatic posts, the consulship at Lisbon or that at New York, 'each of them equal in rank and estimation to the situation of minister plenipotentiary, and I believe both considerably superior in value. . . . My only view [he added] . . . is that of doing him a kindness; and that, if it should on any account not fully and completely meet his wishes, there can be no reason for him not telling me so without reserve, and without the least apprehension of producing any change in my desire to assist him on any other occasion.' Charles did not hesitate. Lisbon was his preference: this 'very lucrative situation' was 'highly desirable in every respect' and likely 'to hold out such pecuniary advantages as must totally remove all difficulties in regard to income'. He declared that 'Your Lordship's long and continued kindness has made me devoted to you for life.' The appointment was confirmed on 9 February 1799 and exactly two weeks afterwards, on the 23rd, Charles and Marcia were married at Cholmondeley House in Piccadilly.

Marcia Lisle was an attractive woman of twenty-three. Dark-haired, with large blue eyes and a graceful figure, she was affectionate and calm in temperament. She made an ideal partner for a husband who, though an amusing and lively companion was sometimes fretful, anxious, and unsure of himself, and they settled quickly into a state of domestic happiness that lasted throughout the all-too-short seven years of their marriage before her tragic death in childbirth in 1806. Those seven years, Charles wrote at the end of his life over forty years later, were 'seven years of the most perfect happiness . . . time has not had the effect of reconciling me to her loss. . . . A more perfect creature never breathed. One more fond of her children this world never saw.'

The new Mrs Arbuthnot was presented at court on 3 April and shortly afterwards Charles and his new wife left for Portugal, and stayed in Lisbon until the end of 1800. When Grenville had offered the consulship in December 1798 he had pointed out that the post was given as a personal favour as 'these situations are not strictly within the course of promotion in the foreign minister's line' and if it became necessary to upgrade the diplomatic representation in Lisbon by appointing a minister Charles could not expect to be given the position. In the summer of 1800 it was judged in London that the war situation required the sending to Lisbon, as Grenville wrote, of 'one who from his station here may evidently have been chosen as being in full and intimate confidence of Government, and able . . . to speak with perfect knowledge of our sentiments, and to impress the Portuguese Government with the persuasion that he does so speak.' The choice fell upon Canning's friend John Hookham Frere, who was sent out to supersede Charles shortly afterwards.

Marcia, first wife of Charles Arbuthnot, 1800. Engraving by S.W. Reynolds, after the portrait by J. Hoppner

Charles was not idle for long. In 1802 he returned to Sweden as envoy extraordinary, in an attempt to woo the Swedes into support for Britain in the event of the resumption of war with Napoleon. He and Marcia settled comfortably in Stockholm, assisted by an extra allowance from the British government which doubled his pay. Their family was beginning to grow. Their first son, Charles George James, had been born on 10 December 1800 on board the navy frigate *Juno* which took them home from Lisbon. Three other children followed, named Caroline, born in 1802, Henry, and Marcia, sometimes called Maria. Charles's mission to Sweden was brought to an end in 1803 when he was recalled and appointed Under-Secretary at the Foreign Office by the new Foreign Secretary Lord Hawkesbury, who later became 2nd Earl of Liverpool and then Prime Minister in 1812, under whom Charles was to serve in the Treasury. Hawkesbury was an intimate friend and political disciple of Pitt, who had resigned the Premiership in February 1801 when George III refused to make any concessions to the Irish Catholics. Henry Addington, another disciple of Pitt but a staunch anti-Catholic, had become Prime Minister: otherwise the new ministry differed little in policies or personnel from the old, except that Grenville and his followers refused to betray the Catholics and remained out of office, finally coalescing with Fox and the opposition Whigs in 1804. Hawkesbury inherited the Foreign Office from Grenville and, like his predecessor, valued and respected Charles, who did not follow his former patron into opposition. Charles later assured him that 'you were the chief instrument of my success' in his diplomatic career. He considered that his experience in the office as well as on diplomatic service fitted him more than any other suitable candidate for the Under-Secretaryship, while his good temper and manners also endeared him to everyone. The two men had known each other since Oxford; they were almost contemporaries at Christ Church though Charles was three years older, and both were prominent on the dinner-party circuit amongst the friends of the government in the 1790s. When Pitt returned to the Premiership in May 1804 Hawkesbury moved to the Home Office and was succeeded at the Foreign Office by Lord Harrowby, another of Pitt's friends.

When the important post of Ambassador to Constantinople had to be filled in 1804 it was to Charles that the Cabinet naturally looked. Hawkesbury first proposed the appointment to the King, and Harrowby confirmed the nomination after taking over the office. Charles was also sworn in as a Privy Councillor, as Harrowby wrote to George III, because 'It appears particularly desirable at this time that your Majesty's Ambassador Extraordinary at the Porte should have all the weight which can be given him by the distinctions usually conferr'd upon those who have the honour of representing your Majesty's person in that rank'.

Charles and Marcia had a difficult journey to Constantinople. It had been intended that they should go by sea, in a Royal Navy frigate, but Charles was then ordered to travel overland to Vienna on the way, where he was to stand in for a few weeks for the British minister Sir Arthur Paget, who had asked for leave to attend to his private affairs at home. It then appeared that Paget did not after all wish to leave Vienna, but the Arbuthnots were marooned there for several months until Lord Nelson, Commander-in-Chief of the Mediterranean fleet, could provide a frigate to carry them from Trieste to their destination. All this, Charles later pointed out in the House of Commons, put him to 'very considerable expense' from his private fortune, since his official salary and expense allowance did not cover the cost. Nor was this all. He discovered while in Vienna that there was no suitable residence in Constantinople for a British Ambassador. Other embassies were housed in palaces, the French one being particularly grand, and for reasons of prestige it was essential for the British to be at least equally splendid and for the ambassador also to have a suitable country residence. A previous ambassador, Lord Elgin, had had to occupy the French palace in the absence of a French mission, but he had been offered by the Turks a site on which to build a palace for which they were prepared to advance the money, and which they insisted should be superior to all the others 'as our court was then, in their estimation, superior to that of the other nations of Europe'. Elgin had begun the building but he was recalled after only the outer walls had been constructed and his successor, Mr Drummond, disliked the country so much that he asked to be recalled and left the work still unfinished.

On discovering this to be the situation, and being told that there was no suitable alternative residence in the suburb of Pera where the foreign missions were located, Charles wrote home to ask for instructions. Harrowby authorized him to complete the building but warned him not to incur large expense. On discovering how costly the completion of the project would be, Charles tried to save the British government's money by selling for £3,000 part of the land donated by the Turks: but, on being warned that his hosts would take offence at his so doing, he had to repurchase it, so adding to the costs. The palace, he later observed, as planned by Elgin, was 'immense, as large he believed as was ever inhabited by a private individual', and as the British government expected him to furnish it himself he had to send to England, at great personal expense, for furniture and household goods. The cost of the building came to over £17,000. He estimated that his travelling expenses and the costs of preparing the embassy for his residence amounted to nearly £6,000, and there were other necessary expenses for messengers and for the presents and bribes expected at the Turkish court. His annual net salary amounted to £6,452 but he reckoned that his expenses were double that sum, though he claimed to have lived as economically as possible. All these circumstances made his position difficult, and he wrote home to ask for his salary to be increased, but without success.

Constantinople was indeed a critical post at that moment in the war against Napoleon which had broken out again in 1803. Towards the end of the previous decade the eastern Mediterranean had become a principal theatre of operations, with Napoleon's conquest of Egypt and Nelson's victory at the Nile in 1798, followed by the British reconquest of Egypt and its restitution as part of the Turkish Empire. A peace treaty between France and the Sultan of Turkey was signed in 1802. Since the beginning of the 1790s the fate of the corrupt and decrepit Turkish Empire, which stretched westwards to the borders of Hungary, south into Egypt and northwards to the Black Sea, had become a question of diplomatic, strategic and economic importance to the three great European Powers, Britain, France, and Russia. British opinion was not sympathetic to the Turks, who were seen as brutal oppressors of the Christian peoples within their Empire, but it was equally important to British interests that the collapse of the Turkish Empire should not enable either France or Russia to pursue their ambitions to dominate the Near East, to the detriment of British trading interests there and the overland route to India. It became British policy to prevent the collapse of the Ottoman Empire and to maintain friendly relations with Constantinople. The integrity of the Turkish Empire was 'a principal object of the policy both of Great Britain and Russia', Grenville, now Prime Minister, wrote in July 1806. Russia and Britain signed alliances with the Turks against the French in 1798–99, hoping to stabilize the area. After the peace of 1802, however, the French began to insinuate themselves into favour at the Sultan's court and the British and Russians were again concerned lest French influence should prevail. The French Ambassador at Constantinople, General Sebastiani, gained powerful influence and it was important for Britain to counter and if possible destroy it. This was to be Arbuthnot's task: but it was an uphill struggle. His task was immeasurably increased by personal bereavement. Marcia had suffered from a long illness at Constantinople in 1805, but she seemed to have recovered and soon became pregnant again; possibly weakened by her illness, she died giving birth to her fourth child on 24 May 1806.

Charles was devastated. 'To me it was dreadful', he wrote in his fragment of autobiography some forty years later. His mother-in-law wrote of 'our most severe privation' in Marcia's loss; 'I trust it may be some relief to your afflicted mind, to know that it has pleased the Almighty to grant me an humble submission to his correction' and she offered to help bring up 'your infant family' in the hope that this might 'fulfill the will of our ever to be lamented Angel'. Charles was later to write that between Marcia's death and his engagement seven years later to Harriet Fane he never knew a moment's happiness. 'During the time that I was there' (in Turkey), he wrote in 1808, 'my mind was rendered inactive & at last broken down by the severest domestic affliction'. His first instinct was to resign his embassy and return home, but the Foreign Secretary, Lord Howick (later Lord Grey) persuaded him to stay to continue his negotiations with the Turkish government. Charles believed that a show of British naval strength would accomplish his task, but his request for a naval squadron to back up his negotiations was refused with what were to be disastrous results. 'The Turks attend to those alone whom they respect and fear', he was to write in 1809, but in 1805 he was expected to achieve his mission empty-handed.

In 1806 hostilities broke out between Russia and Turkey, Sebastiani having prevailed on the Sultan to declare war to expel the Russians from their occupation of two of Turkey's northern provinces. The Russians asked for British naval assistance and the British government ordered Charles to force the Turks to change sides and to expel Sebastiani: when the Turks rejected his ultimatum and refused to give him his passports he took refuge on a British frigate for his own and his suite's safety and a British naval squadron was sent under Vice-Admiral Sir John Duckworth to force compliance and to safeguard the passage of the Dardanelles. Not for the last time this sheet of water was to witness a major defeat for British arms, though as much because of the Cabinet's hesitant and drifting strategic policy, their delays in sending Charles instructions, and the incompetence of their commander as of the inadequacies of their diplomatic representatives on the spot. As the editor of Lord Castlereagh's correspondence remarked, 'I believe it may be said that never was a force, naval or military, destined for a service of such peril and importance, abandoned with such improvidence to the caprices of chance, or despatched with such neglect of all the means calculated to afford a prospect of success to its exertions, as the little squadron sent on this occasion to awe imperial Turkey, and to work a change in the counsels of her rulers.'

Duckworth's instructions were to support Arbuthnot in his attempts to reach a peaceful agreement with the Turks, but if those attempts were unsuccessful 'you are to act offensively against Constantinople.' If, 'as, from a barbarous practice of the Turkish Government', Arbuthnot and his suite were 'forcibly detained' as hostages, their release was to be demanded on pain of 'measures of hostility against the town'. Duckworth was to rely on Arbuthnot's judgement as to whether hostilities should begin, and if he was so advised he should demand the surrender of the Turkish fleet 'with a menace of immediate destruction of the town.' How Duckworth's tiny squadron of eight ships of the line, two frigates and two bomb-ships was to accomplish this armageddon was not specified, particularly as it would first need to force the passage of the Dardanelles, 'hitherto considered as impassable' as was pointed out by Captain Blackwood of the *Ajax*, one of Duckworth's ships. Nor was the attempt to force the Turks to surrender their navy, give territorial concessions to Russia, and to expel Sebastiani likely to succeed without any troops or resources other than the ships and their crews. The only hope lay in 'the supineness and ignorance of our enemy in applying the ample means of resistance they have'. It was a forlorn hope.

On 11 February 1807 Charles joined the expedition on Duckworth's flagship the *Royal George* at the island of Tenedos, which had been chosen as the starting point for the operation. Three nights later the *Ajax*, 'one of the finest ships in the service, with 282 fine fellows' on board, caught fire as a result of the carelessness of the drunken purser's steward and his mate and was destroyed in twenty minutes. It was, Charles wrote to Admiral Collingwood, 'the most dreadful scene that I ever witnessed & in all its circumstances was as melancholy an event as could well have happened'. Despite this catastrophe, on 18 February the fleet succeeded in forcing the Dardanelles against the hostile fire of Turkish ships and shore batteries firing 'immense stone shot, weighing from 300 lb to 800 lb', 2 feet 6 inches in diameter. 'Pretty missile sort of weapons!' as Captain Blackwood remarked. Twelve British sailors were killed and sixty-six wounded, but eleven Turkish ships were destroyed. The British ships then retreated through the Dardanelles again and were joined by a Russian squadron of seven sail of the line and two frigates, but Duckworth refused to attempt a second passage because of the heavy losses already suffered, twenty-nine being killed and 138 wounded on the retreat. Blackwood declared that more could not have been achieved with double the forces available, whereas if the government had responded to Arbuthnot's plea a year ago to send a squadron to Constantinople 'all would now have been well', and 'Arbuthnot would still have swayed the counsels of the Divan, instead of M. Sebastiani, who now is everything.' As it was, the French were now so much in the ascendant and the Turks so jubilant at their success that he thought even an expeditionary force of 20,000 men with artillery and twenty ships of the line would not achieve the objective.

Blackwood paid tribute to Charles's conduct in the affair. He had

Captain (later Admiral Sir Henry) Blackwood, who commanded the Ajax *at Constantinople*

been, Blackwood wrote, 'not only . . . Minister but Admiral – for, without him, I am sorry to say, even what has been done would not have been attempted.' Duckworth, he thought, was inadequate for his command: 'When I know how meanly Mr Arbuthnot has cause to think of his powers of discrimination, deciding, and acting, as well as bearing up against unavoidable casualties, I really feel professionally ashamed.' It was 'to the decision of Mr Arbuthnot (who is equally mild and firm) that we undertook what little was done . . . it was to Mr Arbuthnot, and not the Admiral, we owe many other consequential decisions, even professional ones.' Charles however had suffered for his exertions. He was now dangerously ill with a fever and was taken with his family on board the *Windsor Castle*, one of the ships disabled in the fighting, to Malta and then home to England.

On his return to England in the spring of 1807 Charles decided to give up his diplomatic career. He was granted a pension of £2,000 a year in recognition of his services, but on 20 May 1808 he had to endure a motion of censure in the House of Commons on the government's policy and actions in which it was alleged that he had acted unwisely and precipitately in deciding to call in naval power to force the Dardanelles, that he had been given too much discretionary power, and that the result of the expedition 'reflected on the honour and character of his majesty's arms'. Canning, who was Foreign Secretary in the new government which took office in 1807, joined in the censure on the expedition and its mismanagement, though he did not attack Charles himself and he argued against the House recording a vote of censure on a ministry that had gone out of office, and proposed that the matter be dropped. Charles felt that the motion was unfair and that he had nothing to reproach himself for, but as he was not a member of the House he could not defend himself publicly. The debate ended without any formal censure against him, but it put an end to any hope of resuming his diplomatic career.

Charles's return was a personal as well as a diplomatic disaster. When he took refuge on a British ship he left all his furniture and possessions, including plate, books, and china behind to be pillaged. He estimated their value at £21,000, for which the government allowed him less than £11,000 in compensation. He told the House of Commons in 1812, when his accounts were still outstanding at the Treasury, that he had spent the whole of his private fortune and was still paying off the debts he had been forced to contract to cover the long delay in the government's passing his accounts and refunding his expenses. He reckoned the total expenses of his mission at over £47,000. He calculated that, had he not suffered these losses, he would on his return have had enough capital to buy an annuity equal to the amount of the pension of £2,000 granted by the government, so that he was only receiving compensation for what he had spent on the public service. The House heard him sympathetically and applauded his public spirit. Both opposition and government speakers expressed 'private regard' for him and approved his candid explanation, but the House could do nothing to help him and he had to be satisfied with their good opinions.

In April 1809 Charles began a fresh career. He wished for an office of suitable rank and active business in government, to occupy his mind and divert his thoughts from his personal loneliness and misery. In that month his friend Henry Wellesley, with whom he had exchanged offices in 1795 to begin his diplomatic career, again recommended him as his successor in the office of Joint Secretary to the Treasury. Charles held this office for fourteen years and served two Prime Ministers, Spencer Perceval and, after his assassination in 1812, Liverpool, the former Lord Hawkesbury who had been his superior at the Foreign Office under Henry Addington. It was a close and confidential relationship which brought him to the centre of political affairs.

As his great-uncle Andrew Stone had served the Duke of Newcastle in the mid-eighteenth century, Charles served Perceval and Liverpool in the early nineteenth. He acknowledged his debt to Stone, and believed that he was following in his footsteps, even though he was only a young boy when his great-uncle died. Perhaps he had subconsciously absorbed his political legacy: it was certainly to be his major contribution to British politics.

3   A Marriage 'Made in Heaven'

Charles and Harriet met for the first time in 1807 when she was still a schoolgirl of fourteen and he was forty. He was in mourning for Marcia and did not take much notice of her, but she was attracted to him and she later wrote that she thought 'you had more feeling & a more affectionate heart than any other man in the world'. They lost sight of each other for four years, during which time Harriet fell in love with Captain Capel, who oddly enough was commander of the frigate *Endymion*, one of the ships which had brought Charles away from Constantinople. 'It is true I liked him but I never loved him as I do you,' Harriet wrote in 1813; 'still I did like him'. Capel however did not return her feelings and she was free of any attachment when she next saw Charles in the lobby of the Opera House in the summer of 1811. Charles remembered her and made a remark to her in passing but she did not know him and walked on, saying to her companion, 'Who is that?' The answer was '*Mr Arbuthnot*'. 'You must know I am the *stupidest* person at remembering faces in the world', she later told him; 'I should forget my own if I did not look in the glass every day.'

Their third meeting was at Apethorpe in the winter of 1812–13. Harriet sat in the window of the breakfast-room trying to find the courage to ask him to frank a letter for her to Lady Monson. Members of Parliament had the privilege of free postage if they franked, or signed, the cover, and they were often asked by their friends and relatives to do so for them, to save the cost of postage. Harriet was nervous about asking, but all the other men in the party had gone out. Charles was walking up and down the room, but she hesitated because she thought he did not like her: he had declined to ride with her the previous day and, she later wrote, he had never paid her 'little attentions', like picking up her handkerchief or fetching her a chair: 'I have been so accustomed to be courted and flattered', she wrote, 'that from the most trivial circumstances possible I judge whether a person likes me or not' and those attentions are 'not to be dispensed with from one who is *one's adorer*.' She recollected that the previous night at Apethorpe Charles was standing close to the door when she went to bed and he did not open it for her – 'That was a *heinous crime*.' When, however, she plucked up courage to ask him for the frank he came up and said 'With great pleasure' – and that evening 'I was charmed because you were so afraid I should catch cold, and you wrapped me up in one of your own handkerchiefs.'

When Harriet returned from Apethorpe and told Lady Monson the story of the frank, Lady Monson remarked that she was sure they would end by getting married because Harriet had said in her letter that Charles was the only man there she liked 'and that I thought you perfect'. Harriet replied 'Oh dear no, I dare say he would rather die, he scarcely ever speaks to me.' However, she had fallen in love with him and, she wrote in August 1813,

> I am sure you will believe me when I assure you I never have or never shall really love anyone else, & I feel quite certain with you I shall be as happy as possible.. . . It cannot please me to know that for seven years you have never had a moment's happiness, but it does please me to think that together we shall be the happiest of human beings; yes, I am sure our marriage is made in Heaven, that we have always been destined for each other.

Charles proposed to her and she accepted him in July 1813 and, as her letters show, she was completely in love. Her letters breathe a radiant happiness as well as a playful affection. 'Will you when you speak to me call me yr *very dearest* Harriet?' she asked.

> I should never refuse you anything then . . . Did you kiss your letter while you were writing to me? Our lips have then touched the same paper. How much I wish you were here now . . . I always receive your letters a little after nine when I come in from walking after dinner, & I come up into my own rooms to read them, & when I go down again Edward sometimes says 'Well Harriet I hope it was very agreeable' & I say 'No business of yours Sir'; but what time do you think I answer them? What o'clock do you think it is now? Very near *three*, it is really very wrong but I don't come up to bed till nr twelve & then I generally read yr letter over *nine or ten* times before I sit down to answer it.

She told Charles that her family also approved of him: 'I entreat you not to imagine that my family will do otherwise than adore you'; and 'My mother has just told me there is no one in the world more excellent, no one she likes half as well as yourself & that if she were to consider only her own gratification in the choice of a son-in-law there is not a creature existing she would prefer', but she thought their marriage would be 'madness' because of Harriet's age. However, Harriet was *'quite sure* we shall succeed & I shall be the happiest creature existing'. At her mother's request the wedding would be delayed a short time until Harriet's favourite brother Charles returned to England from Spain: she would be distressed, Harriet wrote, 'at parting with her last and favourite child to any one' and needed time to reconcile herself to the idea. Harriet herself assured him that 'I will never love any one but you, & that no power or entreaty shall induce me to change my present fixed determination.' They were all to meet at the opera that evening: 'I have a great deal to say to you', she wrote, 'but so I always fancy when you are away, and when we are together it all goes out of my head, & I can only lean on your arm & *feel* happy without saying so. What a fool I am! Is it not so?'

Harriet's idyllic happiness was shattered only a short time afterwards when news arrived of her brother Charles's death at Vittoria. 'Oh I am so miserable & so wretched!' she wrote, 'but it is selfish of me complaining & lamenting to you, making you unhappy too; but I cannot help it. Write to me my dearest Arbuthnot; console & comfort me, for indeed my heart is almost broken.' She now understood his feelings at Marcia's death: 'I found your picture when I read your last letter, & closed it shuddering at the conviction of what you must have suffered at parting with her, but you will be happy again now will you not? At least I shall be miserable if I think you are otherwise.' She recommended reading the last stanza of *Childe Harold* which she had found comforting, and assured him that her 'sad loss' would never make her love him less.

Difficulties now arose from the concern of Harriet's family about her engagement, a girl of less than twenty, to a widower of forty-six with four children and no great financial prospects. Harriet's eldest brother Harry who was also abroad in the army wrote to urge their mother to prevent the marriage, and Edward wrote that he could 'see no prospect of happiness in so preposterous a union'. Vere, the fourth brother, knew Charles better and was perhaps closer to Harriet and more aware of her feelings than the others, but even he felt that Harriet's own interests must be realistically considered. Anne was quite prepared to welcome Charles as her daughter's husband but she felt obliged to be guided by her elder sons and when she received Harry's letter in early September she told Harriet that she must break off her engagement. Harriet wrote to Charles to tell him so, and was shocked by the violence of his reaction, verbally at any rate. He wrote back reproachfully and his letter made her wretched. She assured him that her family and friends were not unfriendly to him and that they were only concerned for her interests, and for her future. She was unhappy but she could not indulge her feelings openly for the house was full of people, '& while the tears were forming themselves into my eyes I was obliged to smile & effect gaiety & have the eyes of every one upon me. On Saturday I shall be comparatively happy, for everybody will go away, I shall be alone & able to indulge all my misery.' Her mother too was unhappy, for Harriet had felt obliged to show her Charles's letter and 'she has scarcely done anything but cry ever since. . . . She would I assure you be as miserable as I should were it deferred, I mean *for good.*' Harry too did not deserve Charles's censure:

> he is very fond of me, & he only dreads my being left alone perhaps at an early age without those means of enjoyment which he in his partiality imagines I had a right to look to. Forgive him this feeling, for my sake forgive it & do not dislike one whom I consider almost an angel upon earth.

She wrote to him to declare that 'I *cannot retract.* I have placed everything in the best lights' and no one would change her mind. She tried to assure Charles that all would end well:

> we shall be each other's, I know, I am sure we shall. . . . Do not talk of being again in despair, consider it as *certain* & trust to me for all, I can generally contrive to have things as I like best, & so it will be in this case . . . but I entreat you not again to write me such a letter as I received yesterday for I shall really go out of my senses if you do.

She promised 'I will *never* part with *either* of the rings' he had given her: ' . . . we shall always love each other, & I shall always be yours.'

As Harriet had foretold, the crisis passed for the moment, and her letters became gay and optimistic again. Two days later she described a prank with her friend Georgiana Buckley when Edward bet them each a guinea that they dared not walk round the churchyard at night dressed in white sheets. 'You know it is very dangerous to *dare* ladies, & the consequence . . . was, we instantly procured a pair of sheets & made the *tour*, without falling over the gravestones or meeting with any adventure whatever. I thought myself amazingly bold – & I imagine you will think me very silly.'

She was confident enough to go on to write about their future domestic arrangements. She saw no reason why their marriage should affect the position of his children, their governess, or his servants:

> let everything go on as it is, only take me & my maid in, I must have the latter for she is a treasure I should be lost without. I *entreat* you to make no alteration with regard to your children, remember there *is* a common prejudice against a mother in law [i.e. stepmother]; it is natural, & every act which can be supposed to be mine will . . . be scrutinized with a prejudicial eye . . . [but] I shall do all in my power to ingratiate myself, with the one I have already seen I am sure I shall succeed, for I can generally please when I choose to take the trouble, & I should be in love with him had I a heart to bestow.

In fact Harriet quickly came to be loved by all Charles's children and her arrival in the household made them into a close and affectionate family for the rest of their lives. She approved also of Charles's plans to have a *maître d'hôtel* to supervise their household arrangements:

Wax silhouette of Harriet Fane as a young woman

You know you have *kept house* so long, you *must* understand all about it, & if you really will make me quite happy you will indulge my lazy disposition & you & your maitre d'hotel manage everything without my knowing anything about the matter.

'You know you are to *spoil me*', she wrote, 'at least you may try how we should get on in that way & in return I will give you advice whenever you ask it, & *torment* you as much as you like.' She wished to have her own room

perfectly plain; I have a horror of a bed that has a great deal of *dressing* on it, such as I know is the fashion now, I always suspect it must be dirty. I don't mean that such would actually be the case in your house but I should fancy it. Anything in the world & it is but *clean* will do for me.

Despite all these preparations and thoughts of the future, Harriet like many brides-to-be was struck by a sudden attack of nervousness at the idea of marriage. 'It is very odd, for certainly I like better to be with you than anyone else & yet I can't bear the idea of being married', she wrote:

I can't help thinking when I'm married you won't care for me; you'll be different to what you are now, & then I shall be miserable besides you will be at the Office all day & sleeping all the evening. I wish I was only *fourteen* again, & then you say I could not be married, not but what I dare say I shd have contrived it if you had been polite enough to have asked me, just for the sake of getting from school; but you did not care a straw for me then . . .

The mood passed, but in November the family crisis over the marriage settlement came to a head. The difficulties were in truth more of Charles's making than theirs. He was sensitive to what he imagined was her family's hostility and their disapproval of his lack of social rank and wealth, and also unsure of his own ability to give Harriet the comfort and affluence he thought she needed to have. The family's lawyers' first suggestions for a settlement on her he considered 'ruinous' to himself. He had only his official salary of £4,000 a year, out of which he had not only to support himself and bring up and provide for his children but also to meet the considerable expenses of his position. His diplomatic pension of £2,000 was suspended as long as he was drawing his salary; but if he went out of office or his friends out of government it would be all he had to fall back on, and after honouring all his existing commitments and providing for his sons at Oxford he calculated that he would have only £1,000 a year left, and he felt, as he told Harriet, that he would scarcely be able to buy bread for them both. He was also irritated by her family's inability, or as he saw it their refusal, to make any contribution to Harriet's future security: 'it is

I believe without precedent that that burthen shd fall on the husband when no use whatever is derived from the marriage fortune,' he told Vere. With eight surviving children besides Harriet, her mother was unable to do much, even considering that in 1810 she had inherited her father's estate. Harriet said that she had £6,000 a year and gave £300 or £400 a year each to her nine children and 'she is the very best and kindest mother that ever breathed', but she could not treat Harriet differently from the others. The problem was that the Fanes' lawyers and Charles's trustees were each fighting for the best terms for their side, and Charles, unsure of himself and influenced by his friends, was becoming more and more fretful even with Harriet, whom he accused of breaking her promises to him. It was then decided that Vere and Charles should settle matters between them. 'I have *promised* to abide by Vere's opinion and to be satisfied with what he decides on', wrote Harriet, 'and I must *beg* of you to write no more to me about it.' She urged Charles to make up his own mind and declared she would write no more on the matter, 'but . . . I shall think upon no other subject . . . *you* must settle whether we *belong to each other or no.*' She offended him however by referring to a remark made by Vere to her sister Caroline that Charles had said that Harriet had '*made love*' to him – which was 'a joke on his part, they were laughing at, & quizzing me'. Charles wrote an angry letter, to which Harriet replied that 'I have felt most severely all that has lately been passing between us.' She had reread all his letters after going to bed and 'with bitterness and regret have marked the difference between them and those I now receive': but she had been

> so thoro'ly worried and wretched this last week that my spirits are subdued, I have not been able to bear up against the idea that I am your ruin . . . I sat and cried for an hour before I wrote to you, the depression of spirits that hung on me was such as to make me wish to lie down & die. . . . the clock is now striking four, and I feel no inclination to sleep.

'I regret most extremely that of late our correspondence should have been so disagreeable to you', she concluded: 'I hope in a short time it may be more agreeable, or rather that (from our being together) it may cease altogether.' Charles responded with a more affectionate letter which lifted Harriet's spirits: 'You have written more as *I like*' she declared, and she was sure everything would be resolved, but she had another fit of doubts about her future:

> Now we are getting so near the point I wish myself farther off from it again; you may say what you will about impatience and anxiety for it but matrimony after all is the greatest boon on earth. . . . I have not fixed on any day and shan't think about it till after parliament is up and then it will be according as you behave

whether you are agreeable and *gentle in your manners* (which God knows you never are) indeed I begin to have some scruples of conscience for you know . . . I must promise to obey you or something of that kind; now the idea of obeying you has never entered my head and I can't swear to a story; How can I get out of such a dilemma?

'I very often wish for you', she concluded, 'but not just now for I am *en bonnet de nuit* & look so hideous in that dress that you would certainly request to be let off your engagement.'

The solution to the financial problem was now worked out. Charles should insure his life for £10,000, which would provide for Harriet on his death, and he would ask for no other capital or income for her from her family. Charles however objected to having to pay the insurance premiums himself and proposed that Harriet's mother should do so. This was indignantly rejected by the Fane family. Harriet's sister Caroline wrote that it would be tantamount to paying Charles to take Harriet away from her home, and her mother that 'it would have appeared that I was so anxious for it, that I was ready to *pay him* for marrying my Daughter'. Caroline made Harriet promise not to write to Charles again until the matter was settled, and told Vere that Harriet 'is as convinced as I am of the folly of the engagement she has made, and is *almost* as anxious to break it off *honourably*.'

Under Caroline's influence Harriet now wrote to Charles that she must break off the engagement. Charles at first acquiesced, but when Harriet wrote again to say that she did so because of the ruin it would bring upon him to marry her he wrote more angrily, 'reminded me of the promises I had so repeatedly made to him, sent me extracts from my own letters, accused me . . . of having engaged his affections, encouraged him with hopes and then abandoned him'. She told Vere that she was in truth bound by her promises and must marry Charles if he would not release her: however, the financial squabble had so soured their relationship 'that no happiness could be the result of our union' and her family, at first so favourable towards him, had now completely turned against him. 'I could not marry him without making my mother miserable, and disobliging all my brothers and sisters.' She had talked them out of their first objection, to the difference in their ages, but the financial dispute had turned everything sour. She wrote to Charles that she had 'been unable to resist her mother's tears' and she accepted 'the *iniquity* of my conduct . . . that I have gained yr affections only to make you miserable . . . Think of me as kindly as you can, & let me once more assure you that tho' I have been your torment yet no one upon earth can ever have loved you more than I have.' She assured him that 'my sentiments & feelings with regard to you remain unchanged' and declared that 'I shall mourn over my sorrows in silence & *alone* for [since her brother Charles's death] I have now no friend to communicate all the sorrows & feelings of my heart to . . . I confess that till now I never felt as acutely as I ought the irreparable loss that he is to me. . . . I can only think of the small spot that crowns his deserted grave and feel that I am *"alone on earth"* . . . '. She declared that Charles did not feel for her as she did for him 'or you wd not have sent back my last gifts.' She, however, had fixed the heart he had sent her 'to a *strong* black ribbon that it might last for ever, but you have already broken it, and you must now if you have the inclination wear it by the ribbon which I have worn *round my neck.*'

Harriet's letter brought Charles to his senses and he wrote to assure her that all would be well, 'that we shall have riches in plenty, that it will not distress him in the least to make the required sacrifice of income, that it will not be injurious to his children and that he can easily find the security.' Harriet however had been deeply hurt and blamed Charles for the difficulties he had made and which she said he now confessed to have been wholly imaginary. She again asked Vere to talk to Charles and to decide for her: she was so confused and wretched that she did not know what to do. Her mother was now angry with Charles: 'I had the greatest possible regard for Mr Arbuthnot, and had flattered myself, I should have lived in friendship and happiness with him', but he had acted cruelly and imprudently and his 'fault, through the whole business, has been talking and consulting with every one he met: I really feel so provoked about it, that I am quite out of temper . . . I believe I shall never know peace of mind again till I am in my Grave.' She accused him of extorting a promise of marriage from a girl under-age and of 'listening to all the tittle tattle tales, of every Lord and Lady he met with'.

Other members of the family helped to make peace. Lord Westmorland, who was one of Harriet's guardians as well as her cousin, favoured the marriage – 'he is already your decided friend', Harriet had written in September – and he considered the quarrel a storm in a teacup. 'He laughs at the idea of my being ill with the family, as he is sure we shall all be the best friends in the world', Charles wrote. He agreed to act as a trustee of the marriage settlement, and Vere, Lord Cholmondeley and Lord Sackville to be the others. Charles wrote to Vere that 'I am if possible still more jealous of her fame than you can be. I know how excellent she is – I love her at this moment far more than perhaps any of you have ever been aware of.' He dismissed the objections of his trustees to the proposed settlement and Harriet begged Vere to conclude the business as she wished – 'I shall certainly lose my senses if anything now prevents this marriage,' she wrote. Vere advised that 'the war of words may cease and that every effort may be made . . . to banish both from thoughts & conversations all recent events.'

By Christmas 1813 the misunderstandings and heart-searchings were over, Harriet and Charles were reunited in even greater happiness, and preparations for the marriage began. Back in August Harriet had said that she would rather be married in London than at Fulbeck, where her sister Caroline had been married the previous year. Then, five of her brothers had been there but 'three of that number are now in Spain, one alas! is there for ever, *the one* I wd most have wished for on such an occasion . . . it would excite melancholy reflections.' However, probably to please her mother, she agreed to be married at Fulbeck and the ceremony took place there on 31 January 1814. They spent a short honeymoon at her cousin the 10th Earl of Westmorland's house at Apethorpe, over the Northamptonshire border, which Harriet and her family had visited many times and where they were again to be frequent guests in future years. They were soon back in Charles's official house in Downing Street ready for the new parliamentary session, and Harriet's family were soon reconciled to her marriage. Her brother Harry wrote to Charles from Spain to say that although from a sense of duty to Harriet he had at first opposed the marriage, he hoped that now it was settled 'we should always be upon such terms as persons as nearly connected ought to be; and that I should always be found ready to contribute in any way in my power to its future felicity.' Charles wrote a friendly reply. Harry nevertheless confessed to Vere that he was afraid that their mother would be anxious and uneasy about it: 'God grant, however, that all my fears about it may be *visionary*; tho I am sorry to say, it appears to me, a sort of perversion of nature must occur to make them turn out so!!'

Harry's fears were proved false and groundless. Harriet had written of her marriage as 'made in Heaven', and so it proved to be. Lady Bury met them shortly after the wedding and wrote that 'she is very pretty . . . He is all fire and flames and love, . . . and so very proud of her. It is rather agreeable to see any person so completely happy.' For both of them it opened a period of twenty-one years of delight in each other and in a life which was passed not only in domestic happiness but also among social and political events and activities which they shared. In ways which no one, and neither of them, could have foreseen in 1813, they were to become one of the most prominent and influential couples in England for two decades after the defeat of Napoleon.

4 Home and Family

The Arbuthnots set up house in Charles's official residence in Downing
Street and at the modest and rather plain two-storey farmhouse at
Woodford, near Thrapston in Northamptonshire, which Charles had
purchased after his return from abroad. He decided to put his capital
into land as a more secure investment than the stock market, but he paid
an inflated price for the 600-acre estate, which accordingly never made
much profit, especially as Charles was too busy at first to supervise the
farm in detail and he believed, as he told his eldest son, that he had 'a
succession of bad bailiffs'. Harriet at first thought the house and
grounds 'perfectly hideous' but she devoted much of the time they were
able to spend in the country to improving and extending it, and
particularly the garden and the grounds. She did some extensive
planting behind the house in the winter of 1818–19 and noted two years
later that the trees had 'shot [up] quite immensely'. In 1820–21 she
supervised further clearing of old dead trees and replanting, and making
a walk through the plantation beside the house. 'I really hope in two
years' time this place will be quite pretty', she noted in her journal. She
ordered a thousand laurel bushes and a thousand acacias to plant around
her walks. Three years later she began on the house, moving the
farmyard and buildings a distance away and planning new stables and a
dining-room, to make it 'a comfortable, very small dwelling'. She
planted a flower garden in front of the house and a 'French parterre' in
place of the old farmyard: 'When full of flowers, [it] will be quite
beautiful.' By 1826 the garden was 'full of flowers & very pretty' and
she was hanging the pictures in the new dining-room, with her own
portrait by Sir Thomas Lawrence in pride of place over the
chimneypiece. 'It is reckoned one of Lawrence's best pictures &
excessively like', she wrote, though she was always 'expecting to be
asked whether it *was* like me, as it has now been painted ten years'.
Even allowing for Lawrence's notorious flattery of his sitters, the
portrait shows how attractive Harriet was in her early twenties, and
many people then and later noted how she kept her good looks and
figure until her death. Lawrence's portrait of Wellington, given to her
by the duke, hung in the drawing-room. In 1828 she won £80 on the
Derby and spent the money on a japan cabinet which she painted

herself, and new curtains for the drawing-room 'so as to have made my house here nearly complete'. It was 'a place, which, from having made myself, I am much attached to . . . Mr Arbuthnot left all the ornamental part for me to manage.'

Throughout their married life Woodford was their favourite place and they spent as much of their free time there as they could. There was a good deal of social and family visiting to be done and they settled into a regular round of visits, spending Christmas every year with the Westmorlands at Apethorpe as part of a large house party, and regularly visiting the Sackvilles at Drayton, a few miles away, and the Wellingtons at Stratfield Saye as well as Harriet's mother at Fulbeck, who became very demanding in her later years. They preferred being together at Woodford to anywhere else: 'It is impossible to say how I detest visiting', Charles wrote testily in 1831, when they were summoned to Fulbeck. 'It will be as dull as possible. . . . It wd have annoyed Harriet or I would have refused to go.'

By then Charles had taken to the life of a gentleman farmer whenever his parliamentary duties allowed, and especially after 1823 when he resigned his Treasury post and took a less demanding office. He became interested in farming methods and introducing improvements. Harriet referred in 1820 to his 'farming mania'. He had originally seen the farm merely as an investment, but with Harriet's keen interest in the place he began to give it a greater share of his time. He made a few short visits to other farms to pick up ideas, and in the autumn of 1824 he went on an extensive 'farming tour' as far afield as Yorkshire and Northumberland to improve his knowledge of the subject and to buy stock. Harriet wrote every day to send news of home, of the building and planting and of the proceeds of the sale of their cattle and sheep. She entreated him 'not to stand about in the wet, and catch cold. Remember how liable to cold you are and how angry I shall be if you come back less well than you went.' When he announced that he was going to the market, 'What a man you are amongst all yr farmers!' she wrote. 'Going to Market! . . . I dare say you will smell of sheep for a week after yr return. I am delighted however you seem to enjoy yourself so much.' When he bought a bull he seemed, she jokingly remarked, 'frightened to death from the fear of my displeasure', but assured him that 'I *forgive you*' and insisted on paying for it herself. 'Altogether my dearest love', she wrote, 'you seem to have been enjoying yourself as much as any gentleman I ever heard of for the last ten days, don't however expect you are to have these holidays often repeated, once in eight or ten years perhaps you may be indulged, so make the most of this.' During his absence she had entertained visitors including the Duncannons, her mother and brothers, Charles's daughter

Marcia and her husband – who criticized Charles's mangel wurzels but admired the cows and the turnips – the Duke of Wellington, who sent Charles political news, and 'Lady Harrold (the swearing woman)' who had invited the company to dine and sleep, 'so if I have learnt that elegant accomplishment before I return home do not be surprised'. She was also entertained by a travelling organ-grinder and his monkey who so reminded her of 'Mr Roberts and eats precisely as he does that we were in *fits* of laughter', but otherwise 'the house is very dull without you coming in and out, and I do not like yr being away at all. . . . I have never been away from you so long before . . . since I have been married and I feel quite lost', she wrote. 'You cannot think how much we all miss you or how very desolated I felt when that nasty hackchaise drove off the other night.'

Woodford could be only an occasional country retreat from the strains of office and the flurry of London society into which they were plunged on Charles's return to his duties. It was in that social and political milieu that most of their lives were lived. Charles had an official residence in Downing Street which became their London home until he left the Treasury in 1823. As part of a minor government reshuffle Charles then took the office of First Commissioner of Woods and Forests, which involved the supervision of royal parks and estates, including George IV's ambitious plans for rebuilding various of his royal residences and the parts of London round St James's and Buckingham Palaces. He was allowed to stay in the Downing Street home for a short time as his successor at the Treasury, J.C. Herries, did not want to occupy it immediately, but this could be only a temporary arrangement until they found another house in town. After his appointment to the Woods and Forests they had an official residence in Whitehall Place and in 1828 they acquired a plot in Carlton Gardens, the site of George IV's recently demolished Carlton House, and built a new house which was finished and occupied at the beginning of 1830. 'It will be excessively nice & comfortable', Harriet wrote, '. . . it is very warm, clean & pretty and, when the garden is completed & filled with flowers it will be delightful.' 'I am only afraid of its being *too good*', she wrote to her step-son Charles. The only disappointment was that the King, 'with his usual petty spite', would not allow them to have a private entrance to the park, 'altho' every dirty house in Westminster, looking into the Park, has one' and 'we have *a right* to walk in the park'. However, she persuaded Lord Beresford to give her a key to a gate from the street into the Ordnance passage which made a short cut. The building was financed by a mortgage and with the help of Charles's legacy from Mrs Lisle, his former mother-in-law, who died in 1828.

The legacy, of an estate at Winterbourne in Dorset which was sold for

£22,000, rescued Charles's troubled finances and relieved him of his constant anxiety about future provision for his children. They too received legacies, Charles, the eldest, receiving £9,000 and the Kingston property in Dorset, the three younger children something over £14,000 each. Most of the proceeds of the Winterbourne sale were used to buy back parts of the estate at Woodford which he had had to sell to pay debts. He thus recovered the whole 600 acres which he had originally bought. His eldest son also agreed to lend him 'a few thousands' from his legacy on which he offered to pay 4 per cent interest, the equivalent of investment in the funds, to pay off his remaining debts. He also arranged, with Harriet's consent, that the bonuses on the £10,000 insurance policy which was her marriage portion, a sum of about £3,000, should go to Charles and that the £10,000 should be put in trust for Charles or his children on her death. 'My object', he wrote, 'is that all my children shd be as happy as I can make them, & that my behaviour to them shd be such as to make it their interest – as I know it is their earnest anxiety – that I should live long with them.'

Charles was devoted to his family and took great pains over their education. A resident governess, Miss Townshend, had looked after them after his first wife's death, and after they were grown up she remained with the family at Woodford. Like many anxious parents, Charles urged his sons to devote themselves to their studies at school and at Oxford: 'depend upon it', he told Charles in 1816, 'that if you will continue to work as you tell me you are now doing, you will during the remainder of yr life be glad that you gave up present enjoyment with a view to yr future welfare. . . . If you were well read in History; if you were a quick Arithmetician; if rapidly you cd write good language; & if above all I saw an eagerness in you to make up for lost time & to acquire knowledge, I shd not be so urgent with you to drive amusement from your thoughts.' He confessed that 'I am in agony when I see you take pen in hand' for he was sure that 'those who see yr language in writing shd be saying to themselves how cruelly has this amiable boy been neglected.' Five years later although he wrote of his pride in the good opinions of his son that he had received from his superiors in the army who 'all praise you to the skies. – In short I am in raptures with you', he still thought it necessary to urge him to attend to health, rigid economy, and learning foreign languages and to read him a lecture on the importance of full stops in writing.

Henry, the younger son, was not always in such favour with his father, who felt that he was not making enough effort to do well at school. He might have gone into a diplomatic career and was about to go to St Petersburg in 1821 but the Duke of Wellington urged the

Charles and Henry, Charles Arbuthnot's sons by his first marriage. Engraving by F.C. Lewis, after a drawing by Lawrence

advantage of a university education and he was sent to Oriel, where he seems to have emulated his father in his student days and enjoyed himself.

After their education Charles's wish was that his children should not make 'improvident' marriages but marry into respectable families and 'to worthy objects . . . in this I have set them the example'. His wishes were accomplished: Charles, who was in the army, remained a bachelor until 1833 when he married the daughter of Charles's old friend Sir Richard Hussey Vivian – 'Pray tell Miss Vivian with my love', wrote Harriet, 'that she is coming into a very happy & united family every one of which will do all they can to make her happy'. Henry became engaged in 1829 to Lady Charlotte Scott, daughter of the impoverished Irish peer Lord Clonmel, and though, his father wrote, 'She has not a shilling, and at her father's death she will have no more than £3,000', he declared himself pleased if Henry was happy. Henry's brother wrote from his station at the Cape of Good Hope that he was not surprised 'for he was so frequently in love' and though he had not heard of his latest attachment 'I was sure I should find a Mrs Henry Arbuthnot on my return to England.' Lord Clonmel, however, objected to Henry's 'want of fortune' though, as his step-mother remarked, 'he has 1700£ a year and the young lady has not a farthing'. Her father refused his consent to the marriage but as she was over twenty-one she married without it. Harriet and her son-in-law Henry Cholmondeley attended the ceremony but Charles could not get away from his duties and the bride's father also did not go. He was 'a drunken hunting squire & can't bear Henry because he does not drink or hunt', Harriet wrote in her journal: 'Lady Charlotte seems to have a great deal of character & to be sensible & pleasing and I have no doubt they will be very happy' – as indeed it turned out.

Of the two daughters Caroline was the less attractive. Harriet noted that she was 'not pretty' when she took her to her first London ball in 1820, 'but she is so lady like & so very amiable, I cannot help hoping she is as likely to do well & marry happily as many girls who may have more personal beauty than she has.' Her hopes were to be disappointed, for Caroline never married.

Marcia (or Maria, as Harriet seems to have called her) made the grandest match of the four children. She married her cousin Henry, the second son of the 1st Marquess of Cholmondeley, whose sister, Hester, was the mother of Charles's first wife, Marcia's mother. The bridegroom 'is very amiable & good tempered & I feel no doubt of her happiness', Harriet wrote. It 'has made us all very happy'. They were married at ten o'clock in the evening on 1 March 1825, in the red drawing-room at Cholmondeley House, where Charles had married Marcia's mother twenty-six years and one week before. She 'looked very pretty indeed & went thro' it all with great firmness & composure', wrote Harriet. 'I sincerely hope and believe she will be as happy as I am sure she deserves to be. She is amiable, good tempered and well principled, & I believe it is not possible to have a better character than Ld. Henry has.' After the ceremony the newly-married couple went to visit Marcia's grandmother Mrs Lisle at Kingston in Dorset, and afterwards to Houghton, the Cholmondeley's family seat in Norfolk. Marcia 'came out' for the first time after her marriage at the beginning of May, at a ball given by Mme Lieven, the wife of the Russian ambassador and one of the grand ladies of London society. 'It was a very magnificent fête', Harriet wrote, 'with a profusion of servants in the most splendid liveries'. In the summer they went to Switzerland and on their way back spent three weeks in Paris with Marcia's sister and brother, Caroline and Henry. As Charles was in Ireland with his regiment and Miss Townshend was away, Charles and Harriet now had a rare opportunity to spend some time alone together: '[we] enjoy our solitude *very* much', Harriet wrote in her journal, 'I am sure we [are] as happy alone together as we could have been the year we were married.'

In 1826 Marcia gave birth to a 'pretty little girl', to the delight of Charles and Harriet, but their joy was short-lived for the child died at sixteen months, though by then she had another daughter and in 1829 a son. He died forty years later before Henry inherited the title but his son inherited as the 4th marquess. Charles's family was always a source of happiness to him, especially as Harriet quickly became a close friend as well as step-mother to the children. It was no mean achievement for a girl of barely twenty who suddenly acquired a husband more than twice her age and four children aged between eight and twelve. It shows that she was not only able to make herself liked but that she possessed considerable strength of character, an unselfish nature, and the ability to see and understand the needs of those around her – and, above all, a strong determination to make her husband happy. Her correspondence with Charles, the eldest, shows both a genuine mutual affection and a relaxed and easy relationship that contributed much to the atmosphere of the household. Charles kept a room at their London houses and at Woodford until he married and he was always his father's close confidant, consulted about and informed of all his financial affairs and the recipient of his innermost thoughts. 'The older I grow the greater comfort it is to have you with me', his father wrote in 1828: 'Never father had a better son, & you are the comfort of my life. Indeed I must say that let what will happen to me I have to thank God every hour of my life for having given me such children.' Charles frequently urged his son to be aware of this spiritual dimension. 'I want you to have some disappointments, & some hardships', he wrote to him in 1831.

> It is the good will of God that this shd happen to all men, & I hope it will happen to you in the way that will the least injure your real happiness, & be the most efficacious in disciplining your mind & understanding to take the *right measure* of things (neither too high nor too low) & to view them thro' a true medium precisely as they are.
>
> You have the best of hearts. You have great energy. Great ambition. Great means of succeeding in what you resolve upon. . . . Be persevering; Be sober minded; Be indefatigable in study so as to know & to see to the *bottom of things* as well as their *surfaces*; & under the Blessing of God you will prosper & go (as I wish you) far beyond what I have done.

After Harriet's death in 1834 Charles called even more on the strength his family gave him: 'I got yr letter telling me many truths', he wrote to Charles in September,

> showing to me among other truths that I have many blessings still remaining to me – The Chief of all is that I have such Children as scarcely any other Parent has. . . . I know that the world is full of affliction. I know that it is the good will of God to show to us all that this is not our Resting Place; & I feel that as I am not to remain here for any very long time, even at the longest, it is well for me to be weaned from the World.

Charles's last years after 1830 were years of growing despondency which began with the passage of the Reform Bills and his own retreat from Parliament, increasing financial problems and anxieties over his pension, and finally Harriet's premature death in 1834. He decided to hand over Woodford to his son Charles and for the last fifteen years of his life went to live with the Duke of Wellington, also a widower and, like Charles, an admirer of Harriet. It was the final period of a long friendship between the two men, in which Harriet played a leading part which many, then and down to the present day, thought was at the centre of her life. They were mistaken, for she never wavered in her devotion to her husband: but the duke acquired an importance in both their lives which made this, not a *ménage à trois* in the usual sense, but, as one of the duke's biographers has written, 'a most unusual, subtle and successful essay in triangular friendship'.

5 *The* Beau Monde

In August 1813, a few months before they were married, Harriet asked Charles if he would take her to the Continent as soon as the war was over. 'I should like to go to the Mediterranean', she told him, and especially to Spain to 'shed one tear over the cold grave of my dear brother. Oh! if I thought there was a possibility of my ever doing this I should be so happy!' They did not make that journey, for travel to Spain was difficult and uncomfortable in the aftermath of the war, but in the summer of 1815 after the victory at Waterloo they joined the throng of English visitors flooding to Paris who were eager to escape from over twenty years of almost unbroken isolation from Europe.

The Paris many of them discovered for the first time was a very different city in appearance from London. The British capital, at the

Whitehall. *Engraving by Thomas Malton, 1794*

centre of the richest and most prosperous empire in the world, was expanding rapidly outwards from the old City, still the financial and commercial district, into the 'west end' in the adjoining City of Westminster. Here were found the offices of government, the royal palaces, and the Houses of Parliament. They formed a magnet for the aristocratic governing class who were increasingly drawn to London each year for the parliamentary sessions and the social 'season', when they could introduce their sons and daughters into society. Harriet and her brothers and sisters had paid regular annual visits when her father was a member of the House of Commons, and though as a young girl still under-age she could have only a limited part in that social life she got to know that area of the metropolis well. It was a world of elegant domestic architecture, in which new streets and squares of fashionable brick terraces were appearing almost annually to accommodate the growing middle class of the city and to provide town houses or lodgings in the season for the aristocratic visitors. In Bloomsbury, Belgravia, Pimlico and the area north and west of Oxford Street and Hyde Park speculative builders were laying out estates on the property of aristocratic landlords who greatly increased their wealth by this enterprise. Not only the buildings were modern: the streets were broad, paved with stone, with pedestrian pavements and iron railings, the squares provided with gardens for the residents, and there was street-lighting – gas was about to be introduced – and an organized 'watch' system to patrol the streets and protect the persons and property of the inhabitants from crime. This part of London had the appearance of a new, modern, elegantly classical city.

The contrast with Paris must have struck the English forcibly. Paris was still a medieval city, surrounded by a high wall pierced by thirty-two gates, each guarded by troops, and its medieval streets and buildings were almost intact. There were few pavements, the streets were laid with cobblestones or were simply trodden earth, with gutters down the centre to flush away the débris and sewage of the city. Whenever there was a storm they were liable to be flooded. The Champs Elysées, wrote a visitor in 1815, 'only contains a few scattered houses' and the roads were ankle-deep in mud. The only street-lighting was provided by a few oil lamps strung on wires across the streets. The English painters Benjamin Haydon and David Wilkie noted the contrast even before they reached the city:

> Around London [Haydon wrote], in all directions, are neat cottages – villas – all the various signs of sociality and happiness and comfort. As we neared Paris, everything had a deserted, forlorn, insecure appearance. . . . We entered Paris by one of the most dreadful entrances this side the infernal regions; we were saluted as we entered by one of those ear-ringed, red-capped blackguards, a relic perhaps of the bloody times of the Revolution, with the most accomplished abuse.

His first impression of Paris, 'an Englishman used to the regularity of London streets', was that of 'hopeless confusion – cabs, carts, horses, women, boys, girls, soldiers, carriages, all in endless struggle – streets narrow – houses high – no flat pavements'. Yet that evening they came across the Place de Carousel, to be amazed at 'the bronze Venetian horses' (looted by Napoleon from St Mark's), 'the gilt chariot, the Tuileries, the Russian guard, and the setting sun casting its glory over all, . . . a scene . . . which affects me now, thirty-one years after.' Paris was not without its glories. The Revolutionary Republic and the Napoleonic Empire had adopted the classical Greek and Roman styles in public architecture for ideological reasons, to revive in France the greatness of ancient Rome. Imposing new buildings like the Panthéon, finished in the early 1790s, the huge and imposing Arc de Triomphe, started in 1806 and still under construction nine years later, and the church of the Madeleine were all designed in the style of Rome's great public buildings and temples. Napoleon had begun to glorify his régime with new avenues and buildings. These stood out however in a still medieval city which struck the English as strangely old-fashioned and, in parts, even primitive and dirty compared with London. 'All seems to me quite in extremes', one English visitor wrote, 'the fine things so much above one's ideas, & the rest so much below them. . . . There are several very handsome new streets with side Trottoirs, but . . . the others are wretched in the extreme.' Lady Charlotte Bury thought parts of Paris very magnificent, but Sir Robert Wilson told her 'he did not know; the generality of streets were so narrow and dirty, that he should think more of *Swallow Street* ever after.'

Paris in 1815 was nevertheless a magnet for the English, anxious to escape from their island fortress and to resume the pre-revolutionary habit of foreign travel and sightseeing. When Charles and Harriet arrived in the late summer of 1815, after Charles had been released from his duties in the House of Commons, they found crowds of their compatriots there, and many acquaintances – 'the flower of English society', wrote the susceptible Captain Gronow, survivor of Waterloo, who was in Paris with Wellington's army, 'men of fashion and distinction, beautiful matrons and their still lovelier daughters. . . . The magnificent salons of the *noblesse* in the Faubourg St Germain, and the gorgeous *hôtels* of the ambassadors and ministers of the Allied Powers, were thronged with fair ladies of all nations.' As one of the popular songs of the day put it, 'All the world's in Paris.' The English aristocracy present included Lady Conyngham, the Prince Regent's mistress, and her daughter, and Sir John and Lady Shelley, the latter making herself ridiculous by her obsession with Wellington – she even insisted on riding with him at the great military reviews. There were also Lady Oxford, who gave 'charming soirées' at her *hôtel* in the rue de Clichy, the young bachelor Duke of Devonshire, Lady Charlotte Greville, mother of the diarist Charles Greville, the Sutherlands, the Granvilles, the Grosvenors, and many others whom the Arbuthnots would have known. They haunted the *salons* and theatres of the city in search of amusement. Among the fashionable hostesses were many well-known to the English, such as Mme de Périgord, later Duchesse de Dino, niece of the French statesman Talleyrand, Madame Récamier, reputedly the most beautiful woman in France and also a charming, clever and accomplished hostess, and Princess Bagration 'with her fair hair and delicately formed figure. The Princess', wrote Gronow, 'never wore anything but white India muslin, clinging to her form and revealing it in all its perfection.' The most famous *salon* was that of Madame de Staël, an international figure in European society, a leading intellectual woman of her time, possessed of 'massive determination and energy' and an imposing physical presence: 'a large, masculine-looking woman, rather coarse, and with a thoracic development worthy of a wet-nurse', as Gronow admiringly noted. Her *salon* opened at midnight and was the resort of the *haute ton* of the day. Wellington, who visited and corresponded with her regularly, told Harriet, rather tactlessly, in 1822 that 'she was the most agreeable woman he had ever known.'

The English crowded the *salons* to the exclusion of many of the French, who still smarted from their defeat and resented the presence of so many of the victors. Some of the visitors were disappointed to meet so few of the French. 'All the English in the world are here', complained Wellesley Pole, 'and one detests the sight of them.' The city was full of English and Prussian troops and their officers, who formed a large part of the audiences and gatherings in the evenings.

Besides the *salons* where talk, flirtation and discussion carried on far into the morning, Paris provided a feast of entertainment in the theatres, at the opera and ballet, and at the gaming tables and other forms of dissipation available at the Palais Royal, formerly the residence of the Duke of Orléans. There crowds of officers from the allied armies and 'countless foreigners from all over the world' sought amusement nightly: it was, wrote Gronow, 'the rendez-vous of all idlers, and especially of that particular class of ladies who lay out their attractions for the public at large'. It contained many fine shops, 'the most tempting I ever saw' said Elizabeth Fremantle, 'but it is the scene of everything most depraved in Paris'. The more respectable English, Gronow wrote, 'flocked to the opera, and occupied some of the best boxes'. The ballet featured some of the most accomplished dancers of the time, though their dress – or lack of it – scandalized some of the

English ladies and Wellington himself. At the opera, 'the grand resort of all the fashionable world', the leading singers and the finest spectacles in Europe could be seen. 'Good scenes and dancing; indifferent singing; and full of white cockades and lilies and flags', wrote the critical Mr Speaker, Charles Abbot, who attended a performance. 'The theatre is about the size of the London Opera, but very dirty, and filled with dirty company.' Metternich, Palmerston, and Sir Charles Stuart, the British ambassador, were in the Duke of Wellington's box. The Opéra Comique in the rue Féydau, however, Lady Charlotte Bury thought 'the prettiest salon imaginable', with everything in the best taste and the performances very entertaining. Lady Granville described 'a magnificent ballet, Achille in petticoats, with people in the sea, in the air, and, in short, splendid.' Lady Charlotte was captivated by the dancers – 'the dancing of fairies and graces. . . . I felt my very flesh creep.' At other performances could be seen Madame Grassini, 'La Chanteuse de l'Empereur', the international star of the day. Her fine contralto voice and her voluptuous charms captivated both Napoleon and Wellington and she became mistress to both in turn. At the Comédie Française the great Talma acted as Orestes in *Andromache*, with Madame Mars in the comic after-piece, which Abbot liked better. She also starred in *Tartuffe* at the Théatre Française, in which Elizabeth Fremantle thought her 'quite perfect'. Talma also acted with Mlle George in *Oedipus*: '*hors* the ranting, [he] is magnificent as to dumb show, action, and countenance' thought Lady Granville.

Other daytime diversions included visits to the Louvre, with its magnificent collection of 'the plunder of Europe', as Elizabeth Fremantle remarked, though a beginning was being made of shipping the looted parts of its contents back to their original homes, together with the lions of St Mark's. Lady Charlotte Bury was entranced by 'this stupendous emporium of all that is fine in the arts . . . the immortal Venus . . . the divine Apollo . . . the dying Gladiator . . . and above all these, Diana, the light, the chaste, the cold Diana. . . . ' There were also expeditions to the Tuileries gardens where the orange trees were in full bloom in the summer heat, and to Napoleon's residences at St Cloud, Versailles, and the Trianon, and to the Invalides, all to be admired by eager tourists.

Harriet loved music, the theatre, and the opera and even more the brilliance and conversation of the *salons*, parties, balls and receptions. For a young bride of only twenty-two years old it was a time of heady excitement and intense pleasure, in the company of a husband who returned her adoration. Together they revelled in the delights of a long honeymoon and the company of the grandest society in Europe. Particularly at this moment too, Harriet was able to indulge to the full her developing taste for mixing with the leading politicians of the time. The great statesmen of Europe were gathered there to negotiate and discuss the post-war structure of the continent. Metternich of Austria, Talleyrand of France, with his 'dirty, cunning face' as Lady Granville observed, and Harriet's most admired friend Lord Castlereagh, the British Foreign Secretary, architect of the post-war settlement of Europe, were to be seen nightly in the *salons* and assemblies of the capital, and she made a beeline for their company. Her boldness sometimes shocked the more old-fashioned French ladies: 'The English women [here]', wrote the Contesse de Boigne disapprovingly, '. . . appeared to have thrown propriety to the winds'. She remembered in Talleyrand's drawing-room

> a certain little Mrs Arbuthnot, a young and pretty woman who had set up a claim to the affections of the Duke of Wellington, left the ladies circle, joined the group exclusively of men, leaned against a little side-table, put her two thumbs on it, sprang lightly on to it and remained there with her legs swinging, her very short skirts scarcely lower than her knees. An entire colony of English ladies soon came and proved to us that Mrs Arbuthnot's customs were not exclusively reserved to herself.

Harriet was certainly not 'forward' in this way and disapproved rather prudishly of women who so provocatively displayed their charms, so the story may be an exaggeration, but it is certainly true that she preferred the company of men and serious political conversation to the trivialities of female gossip, and elderly tongues were apt to wag at her presumption.

The social life of Paris for the English was centred on the British Embassy, grandly housed in the great Hôtel Borghese, where, Gronow wrote, 'you were sure to find all the English gentlemen in Paris. . . . Dinners, balls, and receptions were given with profusion throughout the season', and Sir Charles Stuart was 'an ambassador who worthily expressed the intelligence, the amiability, and the wealth of the great country to which he belonged'. Castlereagh, in Paris to carry on negotiations with the other allied statesmen, and his wife Emily were housed in luxurious apartments on the first floor of the building and naturally attended most of the social functions given there. Lady Castlereagh, dressed in magnificent diamonds which were the envy of all the ladies in Paris, who were 'affecting to admire, but looking daggers all the while', gave after-theatre parties which were particularly large, attended by the highest-ranking and most notable people in the city, but mostly by the English and consequently, Lady Granville thought, 'extremely dull'. Castlereagh, Gronow wrote, was 'the pre-eminent star in Paris. He was here, there, and everywhere', and in his

Lord Castlereagh: Lawrence, c. 1810

few daytime leisure moments might be seen walking alone on the gallery at the Palais Royal, simply dressed and without the orders and decorations which glittered on his coat at evening parties and receptions or at the theatre and the opera. He was the favourite next to Wellington but his abominable French limited his ability to socialize: he once described the allied cabinets to Mme Lieven as being 'dans un potage'.

Robert Stewart, Viscount Castlereagh in the peerage of Ireland, eldest son of the 1st Marquess of Londonderry, had captivated Harriet from her girlhood days when she had met him in Ireland where he was beginning his political career. It was he who had inadvertently dismayed her that evening when she had been playing the piano for him and he had casually asked her about the rumour that Captain Capel, her current beau, was going to marry someone else. Despite this inauspicious beginning, she quickly became his admirer. He was clever, accomplished and handsome, over six feet tall, with what Harriet later described as 'a remarkably fine commanding figure, very fine dark eyes, rather a high nose and a mouth whose smile was sweeter than it is possible to describe.' He was an accomplished musician, played the cello with distinction, and possessed manners as 'perfect as those of a high-born polished gentleman'. Harriet was enchanted by his attentions, for he too came to feel strongly attached to her, though he was, like Charles, twice her age. He not only shared her tastes in music and the theatre, but was easy, agreeable, and charming in society. He was, wrote another lady – and there were many who adored him – 'one of those cheerful, lovable, give-and-take persons who are so invaluable' in society. 'His implacable placidity, his cloudless smile, his mildness of demeanour, his love of music, his untunable voice and a passion for singing all the songs in the *Beggar's Opera*', charmed the ladies, to whom in turn he was by no means indifferent, though he remained devoted to his wife and shared with her a genuine Ulster Protestant faith. She, however, was totally uninterested in politics and, like Wellington in a similar case, Castlereagh was drawn to the society of those, like Harriet, whose intelligence and political interests made them interesting and agreeable companions.

Harriet, still a young, inexperienced girl, enjoying her first taste of the glittering society of London and Paris, was fascinated by older men of distinction who would talk about politics and treat her as their equal. She soon came to regard Castlereagh as, next to her husband, 'the best, the most excellent creature that ever lived', as she told her friend Lady Shelley in 1820. Her admiration was undisguised, and so susceptible a man as Castlereagh to female charms responded. She became one of the three most important women in his life, together with his wife and Mme Lieven. When they all returned to London he was a frequent and regular visitor to the Arbuthnots' house in Downing Street during the Parliamentary season. They exchanged calls, dined at each other's houses, and visited each other in the country. In town he visited them at breakfast almost every day, jokingly calling his visits 'coming to take his orders', talked to her of the debate the night before, and discussed business with Charles. He and Charles were close associates, for in addition to the laborious office of Foreign Secretary Castlereagh was leader of the House of Commons and in that capacity he relied much on Charles's ability to muster and keep together the majority behind the government front bench. Charles later recollected, in old age, his 'greatest regard and affection' for Castlereagh:

> in private life his kindness and good temper were exemplary and never failing, and . . . in his public capacity truth and honesty of purpose were at all times his invariable characteristics, . . . his mind being totally free from all sinister and selfish feelings. . . . And in truth absence of all vanity and perfect simplicity of mind always characterised him.

After his death, Harriet noted that Charles 'was the person in the world that Ld. Londonderry [as Castlereagh became] loved & trusted the most, in whom he reposed the most complete & entire confidence, & in whose welfare & prosperity he always expressed the most affectionate interest.' As with the Duke of Wellington, Charles shared in Harriet's friendships with other men and played an important part in these relationships. Even Wellington took third place. Next to her marriage, Harriet's intimacy with Castlereagh was the greatest source of her happiness in public and private life. Their presence all together in Paris in 1815 made it a perfect experience for a young bride who was as fascinated by high politics as she was charmed by elegant society and agreeable conversation.

The Arbuthnots stayed in Paris for six months, Charles sacrificing his duties at the Treasury to his new wife's social ambitions. Back in London, though Harriet could not be a society hostess on a grand scale, for she and Charles were relatively poor in comparison with the Lady Jerseys or Hertfords, she used her intimacy with Castlereagh and Wellington, whom she had also encountered again in Paris, to gain entrée to fashionable circles where she could indulge her passion for politics. This fascination may, however, have blinded her to the impression she sometimes gave to others of being too forward in hunting out and monopolizing the attention of important men. It may also have closed her eyes to the nature of her attraction to other men. She was a beautiful young woman, married to an older husband who was also an agreeable conversationalist and popular in society but who did not entirely share her taste for parties and who valued more domestic comfort after his day's, and evening's, labours in his office or in the House of Commons. Gossip began to whisper and scandal to link itself to her name. These rumours almost certainly were without foundation, but they did little credit to Harriet's sense of discretion. In fact it is very likely that she had little interest in sexual relations, and none in the case of men other than her husband. She was even rather prudish in temperament, as several entries in her journal show: she was disgusted at the Duke of Rutland's in 1825 to see the Duke of York, aged sixty-two, making eyes at the Duchess of Rutland, 'an old Grandmother, it is really disgusting', and shocked when the conversation turned on what ladies wore when they rode and it appeared that some wore nothing below the waist but Cossack trousers, whereas she wore three layers of petticoats under her riding habit. Later in the same year she castigated Lady Strachan, 'one of the most vulgar women I have ever met with, having all the pretensions of a fine lady', who was, as Charles Greville remarked, a notorious 'very infamous and shameless woman' who was also depicted in contemporary prints as having an affair with Lady Warwick. She was the mistress of the aged Lord Hertford, and allowed him to speak to her of 'things that a woman never speaks of but to her husband, & not always that (such as the building of water closets in the house)' and wore 'her clothes off her shoulders, short petticoats, & crosses her legs so as to shew up to her knees. She makes me blush often to be in the room with her.'

Infidelity to Charles probably never crossed Harriet's mind, but she never seems to have asked herself what construction others might put on her conduct. Whether Castlereagh, for whom she never made a secret of her adoration, might have developed a physical attraction to her is not certain, but it cannot be considered unlikely. His wife, though devoted to him, had become rather stout and she was generally considered dull in society. Like Wellington, Harriet's other admirer, Castlereagh had a wife who cared little for politics, which filled his life, and who did not sparkle in society or enjoy the company of his friends. She also dressed eccentrically: she had the odd habit of wearing her husband's garter ribbon in her hair. Lady Granville unkindly described her at the Hôtel Borghese as surrounded by 'oriental luxury, she fitter for Wapping'. Harriet, by contrast, was an attractive and intelligent woman who was fascinated by politics and loved to know its secrets. There is no suspicion of what Harriet would have called 'impropriety' in their relationship but she considered Emily to be uninteresting and there was an element of jealousy in Emily's attitude towards her, as Harriet recorded in her journal two years after Castlereagh's death. Harriet believed Castlereagh to be 'the kindest and most affectionate of husbands' but she thought his marriage unsuitable and, consciously or not, seems to have considered herself as occupying part of the place that his wife should have filled. It may not be fanciful to imagine that Castlereagh's mental breakdown in 1822, though primarily the result of overwork, mental stress, and a history of what seems to have been a form of psychotic depression, was in some way connected with his relationship with Harriet. It was her disclosure to him of the anonymous letter she received which seems to have triggered off his anxieties about those he had been sent, and it was to her that he turned when it happened.

In the summer of 1822, Castlereagh's behaviour began to alarm his wife and his friends. Exhausted by the strain of his office and his parliamentary duties, he began to suffer from paranoia and delusions. He fancied that some anonymous letters addressed to Charles and accusing Harriet of an affair with the Duke of Wellington, were directed at him, and he linked them to similar letters he had received over the past three years. He visited Harriet, 'took my hand & entreated me in the most earnest manner to tell him whether I had ever heard anything against him, said he considered me as one of his greatest friends & thought I should have no false delicacy in telling him if I had ever heard anything against his honour or his character.' Harriet laughed at the idea and assured him that although he had a reputation as a flirt 'and very fond of ladies' this was hardly a great crime. He told her that during the last three years he had received anonymous letters 'threatening to tell of his having been seen to go into an improper house'. He became obsessed with the notion that he was being blackmailed for a supposed homosexual encounter, that the Duke of Wellington and the Cabinet were conspiring against him, and that his horses were being prepared for him to flee the country. His words and appearance on his next, and last, visit so alarmed Harriet that she burst into tears and cried almost the whole time he was with her: 'He seemed affected at my crying, asked me if I was displeased with him, whether he had ever offended me (God knows he never had)' and left 'and the door closed for ever on my dear and valued friend'. A few days later he became confused and incoherent and told his doctor that he had committed 'the most horrid crimes' and that everyone was conspiring against him. He even accused his wife of being in the conspiracy, and when she rushed to fetch his doctor he ran into his dressing-room and cut his throat, falling dead into the arms of the doctor as he entered.

Harriet was at Woodford when the event happened. She was so distraught that she could not go to his funeral in Westminster Abbey, but went three days later to weep 'tears of bitterness and unavailing sorrow' over his grave. For several weeks she could not bring herself to write of it in her journal and when she finally sat down to do so she poured out her agony on the paper. 'I have been stunned by the dreadful blow that has . . . robbed me of the dearest & best friend I had on earth', she at last managed to write. He was

the man who, for eleven years that we have been known to each other, has taken the most affec^te interest in all that was a subject of joy or sorrow to me, who from the hour I married to the day of his death has been the kind & affectionate adviser to whom I have ever had recourse in every annoyance, and whose place in my fond remembrance I feel can never be filled up. . . . Nothing ever happened to me of importance, either private or in our public situation, I never had any annoyance or distress that I did not consult him & receive from him the most friendly advice and the kindest sympathy. [He was] a great and amiable man, respected for his private virtues . . . & loved to adoration by his family & friends. . . . It was impossible to look at him and see the benevolent and amiable expression of his countenance without a disposition to like him, & over his whole person was spread an air of dignity & nobleness such as I have never seen in any other person. . . . His tastes were simple, he was passionately fond of music, fond of flowers, of his farm, full of kindness for his servants and of charity for the poor, adored by his whole family.

After his death Harriet could no longer bear to live in Downing Street, opposite the Foreign Office 'where he no longer presides', or to see the house in St James's Square where they used to visit him: 'the place he always occupied on the sofa will incessantly remind me of the happy hours I spent with him and which will never return.' At Woodford she found a print, 'a striking likeness', engraved from one of Lawrence's portraits and she spent hours 'in mourning over that shining countenance, the image of what he was in his hours of relaxation and happiness'. There was now a void in her life which even Wellington never completely filled, though it left the duke as her closest personal and political friend. Wellington too saw himself after 1822 as Castlereagh's political legatee and guardian of his principles and this drew him even closer to Harriet and Charles. 'He has promised to fill the place of the friend I have lost', she confided to her journal a week after the funeral. That association was to be the second great feature of her life, and one may imagine that Castlereagh's fate did something to influence its character.

6 'The Beau'

Charles and Harriet's nineteen-year friendship with the Duke of Wellington is the best-known feature of their lives. It became central to Harriet's existence in 1822, but by then the duke was no recent acquaintance. He had known her and her family since she was a child, and there were many connections between their families. When still plain Arthur Wesley, before his elder brother changed the family name to the more aristocratic-sounding Wellesley, he had served as one of the aides-de-camp to Harriet's cousin the 10th Earl of Westmorland as Lord Lieutenant of Ireland in the early 1790s: Westmorland's son Lord Burghersh served on Wellington's staff in the Peninsula and took part in the battles of Roliça and Vimiero. In 1811 he married Wellington's favourite niece Priscilla Wellesley-Pole and in 1815 he was one of the duke's aides-de-camp at Waterloo. Harriet's eldest brother Henry was also an aide-de-camp in Dublin in 1793 and commanded a cavalry division in the Peninsula, where two of her other brothers, Charles and Mildmay, also served. Harriet as a child must have met Wellington in Ireland before he left to make his career and reputation in India and they met again in London in 1814, soon after her marriage. When Harriet and Charles arrived in Paris the following year Wellington was already there, the hero of Waterloo and the toast of all the town, and they were inevitably thrown together in the same circle, with the Castlereaghs and other prominent British visitors. Harriet was under Castlereagh's spell but she also found Wellington attractive and was fascinated by his stories of campaigns and battles, which he was always very willing to tell to the company. The duke, however, was almost monopolized by Lady Shelley, who was jealous of any other company and was fulsome in her adoration.

Charles too was a close associate of the duke, as he was of Castlereagh, and he had many political and personal connections with the Wellesley family. In 1809 he had helped to bring Wellington's nephew into the House of Commons and in the previous decade, before he knew Harriet, he had been a colleague of Wellington's younger brother Henry Wellesley and they became close and lifelong friends. Contrary to the suggestions of some modern commentators, and in a similar vein to Harriet's friendship with Castlereagh, Charles was not a

The Duke of Wellington: Lawrence, c. 1815

mere onlooker in the relationship between his wife and the duke, but at least an equal participant in bringing them together. He shared Harriet's admiration of the duke's political principles and conduct and became one of his devoted associates. The relationship was that of the sides of an equilateral, not an isosceles triangle.

Several biographers have written of the Duke of Wellington's character and personal life. Born Arthur Wesley in Ireland, on 1 May 1769, the fourth surviving son of Garret Wesley, Lord Mornington, he was brought up in the frivolous society of the Anglo-Irish Protestant aristocracy, a lifestyle occupied with hunting, horses, drink, dancing and gambling, and occasionally politics. He was sent to Eton in 1781 but his father died the same year and money was short. As Arthur was reckoned to be the dunce of the family and his brothers were clever, he was removed from Eton three years later and taken by his mother to Brussels for a year. He learnt little at either place. He was lonely and shy, idle and lethargic, refused to take part in any games, and suffered from frequent colds. His mother was perplexed as to what to do with him and so sent him at the age of seventeen into the army, where the less able sons of the upper classes, provided they could ride, and provided their families had money and influence, could rise to senior positions without the necessity of talents or intellect. His eldest brother Richard, the future Marquess Wellesley, destined to be Governor-General of Bengal and for a short time Foreign Secretary, obtained a commission for him and a post as aide-de-camp to the Marquess of Buckingham, the Lord Lieutenant of Ireland.

Arthur now developed rapidly in self-assurance and social accomplishments. He was described as 'handsome, fashioned, tall and elegant'. The viceregal court at Dublin provided a fashionable and stimulating environment and 'brought him out' – and also gave him the leisure and inclination to begin to educate himself by reading and private study. In 1790 Richard secured a seat for him in the Dublin Parliament and he was launched on what seemed likely to be a political career. In 1793, however, Britain went to war with France and Arthur joined his regiment. He took part in the Duke of York's ignominious campaign in the Netherlands in 1794 but there was little scope for military activity after that until 1796, when his regiment was ordered to India and he sailed in June.

India was the making of Arthur as a soldier and of his career and reputation. He stayed there nine years, and learnt the art of war by practical experience. He distinguished himself by a number of victories over the French and their Indian ally Tipoo Sahib, notably at Seringapatam and Assaye. He was given a knighthood of the Bath, and acquired a modest fortune from the spoils of war. The Indian climate took its toll, however, and he returned to England in 1805 to restore his health. Back home, as a 'Sepoy General', his military status was relatively low and his part in another abortive and mismanaged expedition to north Germany did nothing to improve it. He returned to politics, obtained a government seat in the Commons, and in 1807 became Chief Secretary in Ireland – the Lord Lieutenant's right-hand man and Irish equivalent of Charles in London, controller of patronage and government manager of the contingent of Irish MPs who were sent to Westminster to represent their country in the Imperial Parliament. He did not give up the army however. He retained his commission and took part in the successful expedition to Copenhagen in 1807 and was made a lieutenant-general.

In 1808 began his most famous military assignment apart from the command at Waterloo seven years later. He was sent out to the Iberian Peninsula as part of the force designed to support the Spanish and Portuguese uprisings against the French conqueror, but as a relatively junior officer and lacking previous experience of fighting the French in Europe he was subordinated to elderly and over-cautious commanders who threw away the advantages gained by victory, so that the expedition failed to achieve its objectives. A few months later however he persuaded Castlereagh, the Secretary for War, to send him back to Portugal, commanding a force of 20,000 British troops, so beginning the initially defensive but ultimately successful Peninsular campaign which demonstrated beyond question his brilliance as an army commander. A succession of victories saw him advance in rank and title, to a viscountcy after Talavera, an earldom after Ciudad Rodrigo in 1812, a marquessate after Salamanca, a field-marshal after Vittoria in 1813, and a duke in 1814 two days after his forty-fifth birthday and on the eve of his entry into Paris to head the grand victory parade before the restored King Louis XVIII. Just over a year later the victory at Waterloo sealed his military reputation for ever, and heralded his return to British politics and society.

Wellington in 1815 was moderately tall, slender and straight-backed, with a thin face, brown hair, clear blue eyes and the famous hooked nose. Even more than Castlereagh, he was surrounded by pretty women whose company he enjoyed and who sought him out eagerly. Harriet wrote that in Paris 'the adoration of the ladies for the Duke was given the name "*la nouvelle religion*"'. He had the reputation of being a ladies' man since his days in Ireland, and throughout his adult life the nickname 'the Beau' stuck to him. Though he remained a bachelor until his return from India he had no shortage of female company and there were several affairs, some of them with married women. He treated these as a diversion, rather than committing himself to anyone. Some of his relationships were platonic, but others were not, and the world, not always able to distinguish between the two categories, often assumed the latter. In fact Wellington required from his women friends many different qualities. In some cases, such as that of the famous courtesan Harriette Wilson, who told all – and possibly more besides – in her scandalous *Memoirs*, sensual gratification was the sole purpose. From others however he sought intellectual or domestic companionship, neither of which he could find in the wife he had unwisely, if honourably, married in 1806.

She was Kitty Pakenham, a daughter of the Irish peer Lord Longford, with whom he had fallen in love as an inexperienced young man in Ireland when he was aide-de-camp to the Lord Lieutenant. She was in fact a childhood friend, for the two families lived a short distance apart, but her father disapproved of Arthur as a suitor because of his lack of prospects and he refused his consent to Arthur's proposal in 1793. He nevertheless remained true to her, for she was young, attractive, lively and shared his liking for books and music, though neither was an expert performer. (Arthur loved the violin in his youth but when he entered the army he had burned it.) Arthur nevertheless considered himself committed to Kitty and throughout his years in India avoided any relationship with any other woman beyond his occasional flirtations, which may have been more serious for the ladies than they were to him. During his stay in India he received occasional news of Kitty, whom her family had tried unsuccessfully to marry off to Lowry Cole, son of the Earl of Enniskillen, another soldier but one with better-looking prospects. The affair ended when Cole was sent to the Mediterranean in 1801. Arthur still remembered Kitty with affection and though etiquette forbade him to correspond with her he wrote to a friend in 1804 that his 'opinion and sentiments respecting the person in question are the same as they have ever been'. When he returned to London, in the midst of his affairs with Harriette Wilson and several others, he wrote that 'She has my promise and my honour demands that I should keep it.' Her family's objections having been long since withdrawn, he renewed his proposal and they were married in April 1806 in Dublin.

He knew that it was a mistake by then, but he was too honourable to withdraw. She had had the smallpox and lost her beauty – 'She has grown ugly, by Jove', he muttered at the altar to his brother Gerald, who married them. Furthermore, Kitty had remained shy and remote, hated politics and society and hardly ever went out, and yet was incompetent as a housekeeper and had no idea how to manage her allowance. She was 'good, worthy, sweet and quite useless to him' as a companion or probably in any other way.

He told Harriet the whole story in June 1822, when they walked in a

Catherine, Duchess of Wellington, at her easel: J. Hayter

friend's garden one evening after supper. He 'complained bitterly of the distress it was to him to be united to a person with whom he could not possibly live on any terms of confidential intercourse', she wrote in her journal.

> He assured me that . . . she did not understand him, that she could not enter with him into the consideration of all the important concerns which are continually occupying his mind, and that he found he might as well talk to a child. . . . He told me . . . that his tastes were domestic, that nothing w^d make him so happy as to have a home where he could find comfort; but that, so far from that, she made his house so dull that nobody w^d go to it . . . & that it drove him to seek abroad that comfort & happiness that was denied to him at home. [He added that] I must have seen how much he preferred to any other the quiet visits that he paid to us at Woodford, how eagerly he always accepted our invitations, because he felt that he could do as he liked, that he could ride & walk with us & discuss with us any subject that occupied him; but that, at his home, he had no creature to speak to, for that discussing political or important subjects with the Duchess was like talking *Hebrew* to her.

Harriet expressed her astonishment 'at his having married such a person' and laughed at his confession that he had been 'a *d—d fool*. I was not the least in love with her. I married her because they asked me to do it & I did not know myself . . . &, in short, I was a fool.' He went on to tell her the whole story of his courtship and, she wrote, 'He seemed quite *soulagé* after having made me this confidence, & seemed quite glad to have someone to whom he could say anything.'

This conversation in the moonlight of a late evening in June, two months before Castlereagh's suicide, is the key to Harriet's relationship with the duke. It was certainly not a sexual relationship. The evidence of Harriet's journal, of her letters to her husband, and of her life and character in general, is clearly and unequivocally against it, though gossip sometimes suggested otherwise. It is even more inconceivable that a man of Wellington's honour and character could seduce the wife of a close friend and trusted associate, as Charles was. Harriet sometimes behaved indiscreetly in the eyes of the world in treating the duke in so proprietary a manner, walking out on his arm and looking at him affectionately, ostentatiously seeking his company in public assemblies and places and visiting him or receiving his visits when Charles was not there, though she denied any impropriety. On the vast majority of occasions when they met in public, she wrote, 'I always have my daughters, their Gov^{ss}, generally Mr Arbuthnot & my brothers & so many men that it is a joke against [me] that half my people spend the night in the passage', and in private 'I never receive him but when my door is open to the whole town unless Mr A. is at home & chooses we sh^d be a trio.' She was distressed on two occasions, in August 1822 and in April 1824, when anonymous letters accused her of a sexual affair with the duke. On the first occasion it was the spiteful work of an unsuccessful suitor to Charles for an office in the government service, on the second it was Charles Greville, the diarist, who was angry because he found out that the duke had had an affair with his mother. 'Luckily my dear husband & I', she wrote, 'live upon terms of such affection & confidence that these base insinuations have only the effect of making us abhor the wicked feelings which could prompt anyone to write such a letter.' They discussed the letter with the duke and agreed to ignore it, but she realized that she must be more discreet in future and she and Wellington 'agreed that in public we will not talk much together, but go on just the same in private'. Harriet's journal was kept strictly under lock and key, she refused on at least one occasion to allow even Castlereagh to see it, and certainly did not write it for future disclosure to anyone, so that there is no reason to doubt the truth of what she wrote.

Her love for Wellington was genuine but platonic. Their common friend the Spanish General Alava, being questioned in 1826 by a jealous Lady Jersey, as Harriet recounted, 'whether the Duke was *in love with me!*' replied that it was *'la liaison la plus pure au monde, . . . c'est l'amitié toute pure, et j'en suis enchanté, car cela le rend parfaitement heureux.'* 'I told Alava that I was delighted that he did me justice', wrote Harriet. 'The Duke's friendship for me & Mr A. has just been what it now is for the last ten years and, unless she wants the Duke as a lover herself (which I suspect she does) it can be no concern of hers. It makes me uncommonly angry.' Lady Shelley, who knew them both well, entirely dismissed such allegations on their relationship: 'I, who knew them both so well, am convinced that the Duke was not her lover. He admired her very much – for she had a manlike sense – but Mrs Arbuthnot was devoid of womanly passions, and was, above all, a loyal and truthful woman.' Though Harriet could write in 1824, when Wellington was ill, that 'His life is so precious, & he is so inexpressibly dear to me', it was an expression of love as profound friendship rather than as sexual passion.

Wellington, despite his earlier reputation as a ladies' man, was equally concerned for the propriety of his friendship with Harriet. He had never in fact been promiscuous amongst his social acquaintances, though he had taken advantage of his opportunities with courtesans like Harriette Wilson. When she wrote her supposed memoirs for the purpose of extracting money from men she named as her lovers, the duke, who featured prominently in them, told her to 'publish and be damned'. When she did so, Harriet was quite unimpressed. 'It is great nonsense', she wrote to Charles. '. . . What she says of the Duke is so ridiculous & so unlike him that I shd doubt her knowing him except for his generosity in giving her money.' In this she may have allowed her affection to rule her judgement, but her own knowledge of the duke certainly predisposed her to think him innocent. She went on to tell Charles of General Alava's remark that *her* friendship with the duke was always '*la conduite la plus parfaite*' and that 'tho'' everybody saw how intimate I was with the Duke, & how much he admired & liked me, & tho'' he had the reputation of always *faisant les grimaces aux femmes*, no creature ever imagined the possibility of an impropriety in it. I hope this will please you, dearest', she added.

What the duke wanted from Harriet and Charles was above all companionship, the opportunity to relax in confidential conversation, to unburden his thoughts and anxieties before friends who would tell no one else and who would give him sympathy, understanding and domestic comforts. They gave him, in effect, a home. He valued too their political advice. He once described Harriet in a letter to Charles as 'a pattern of *sensible* women' and he often asked, and even more often received, political advice from her. Henry Greville, Charles Greville's younger brother, wrote in 1834 that the duke's intimacy with the Arbuthnots over twenty years 'has been his greatest resource . . . I believe him to be equally attached to husband and wife and there was no matter personal or political in which he was concerned or interested that he did not freely discuss with them in the most unreserved manner.' As Lady Salisbury wrote at the same time, Harriet was 'a tried and valued friend to whom he was sincerely attached'.

On her part, Harriet confessed her feelings to her journal in 1830:

> I sometimes think it is most unfortunate but it is quite true that, excepting my husband & his children, I have no feeling of warm interest for any human being but the Duke. There is something about him that fascinates me to a degree that is silly, but which I cannot resist. He is so amiable, so kind hearted with a degree of roughness, & so frank, that I always feel I wd die for him . . . & it makes me miserable to think he shd have anything to vex him . . . except the Duke, none of the public men interest me.

Ten years earlier she had written of a four day visit the duke made to Woodford that 'nothing could be more amiable & delightful':

> It is quite refreshing to be in constant and habitual intercourse with a mind so enlightened & so superior as his is, which is familiar with every subject and which, at the same time, can find amusement in the most ordinary occupations of life. . . . He talked of his political & military life, & nothing could be more amiable than his manner of describing his feelings after each successive battle, when all ideas of triumph & gratified pride were lost in his regrets for the friends and companions that those triumphs had cost him. He is as excellent in heart as in mind, & may God preserve him to us! for without him we shd all go to ruin!!

Again, three years later, the duke 'was, as usual, charming. He is the pleasantest person possible in a house, he is so simple & so easily amused & pleased. We rode & walked & drove in his curricle every day, & I shall miss my agreeable companion very much.' 'It is impossible to know him well without loving him', she wrote in 1826.

Their close friendship began in Paris in 1815 and within three or four years their future relationship was established. It was not all serious politics. The duke jokingly christened her 'La Tyranna' in writing to their close mutual friend, Frances Lady Shelley, who corresponded with them both, and Harriet and Frances retaliated by calling him 'the Slave'. Their letters were often playful and facetious, Wellington claiming to Frances that he was not allowed by 'la Tyranna' to write to or visit her without permission – on one occasion the permission was 'peremptorily refused. The truth was that our temper was a little disturbed at the moment, about something I had said about women and children, and in consequence of my riding slower downhill than was liked!!' In the following year (1820), 'I can tell you that my tyrant was by no means satisfied with you for not having applauded her *good nature* in allowing me to go the last time to Maresfield [Frances's home], and she swore she never would permit me to go again. However, I'll try. In the meantime, "*when the cat's away the mice go and play*", and as she is at her brother's in Lincolnshire . . . I have taken leave to invite you to Stratfield Saye, where I hope you will stay as long as you will like it.' And later, 'Black Cap' (another nickname for Harriet) 'is, in my opinion, quite right not to give me permission to quit her too frequently.'

Serious matters intruded sometimes, however. In February 1820 the 'Cato Street conspiracy' by a group of radical extremists to murder the whole Cabinet at dinner was betrayed and the conspirators arrested. Castlereagh and Wellington were among the intended victims, and Harriet wrote off at once to Frances, beginning 'I cannot write to you today in a style of *badinage* about 'the tyrant and her slave', for, in truth, I have had such a fright about him and all those I love best almost in the world.' How, she asked in her journal, could such a plot be conceived against the duke, 'whom every English person ought to worship'? The duke laughed it all off and they resumed their companionship in mutual visits to Woodford or back to Stratfield Saye, or in London between Apsley House and Downing Street, and on the country house circuit, which the duke called 'a scamper about the country', in the autumn and winter when Parliament was not sitting. Then there was time for parties, for the duke to shoot (usually very badly, especially when Harriet teased him), and for quiet domestic gatherings around the fireside. The duke admired the progress of the farm and garden at Woodford and the Arbuthnots likewise admired his attempts to make Stratfield Saye more comfortable. They usually spent Christmas together at the great Westmorland house-party at Apethorpe and moved on to spend the New Year with the Rutlands at Belvoir. Their relations were never closer or more intimate than in the period after Charles's change of office in 1823 – Wellington told Lady Shelley in June 1824 that 'I am . . . more a slave than ever, and the Tyranna more tyrannical!' Harriet on her part remarked that 'the Duke . . . seems never to do anything without communicating with Mr Arbuthnot and me.'

When the Arbuthnots settled into their new London house in Whitehall Place, the duke visited them regularly while they were in town, and he frequently came to Woodford during breaks from official duties. They occasionally went to Stratfield Saye, but Harriet disliked the house and Wellington preferred to avoid his wife's company there if his friends were able to receive and entertain him. Harriet remained friendly with Kitty, but they had even less in common than the duchess did with Wellington and Harriet wrote in 1826 that she was 'the most abominably silly, stupid woman that ever was born'. The duke, as he said on one occasion, regarded the Arbuthnots' house as his true home and was never happier than when in their company, or that of Harriet when Charles was not present. Harriet for her part loved to talk politics, to hear the duke's stories of his military exploits, and to feel herself to be his adviser and, occasionally, to use him to advance her own views. It was delightful, she wrote, to hear him speak of his campaigns – 'His countenance lightens up, his eyes flash fire & his whole appearance is as if he was inspired.' When he left on a diplomatic mission to St Petersburg in 1826 she was the last person he came to see and he said she should be the first he would visit on his return, and he made her promise to write to him twice a week. It was an example of a rare but, when successful, mutually satisfying relationship, and it enabled Harriet to fill her journal with the political gossip of the day. She, Charles, and the duke agreed about almost everything in political, social and private life and for all of them this was a period of fulfilment never matched at any other time. The duchess stayed most of the time at Stratfield Saye or in Ireland, a lonely and neglected figure. In 1827, when Wellington and Charles were temporarily out of office, the duke dined on his birthday with his two friends, 'this year quite alone', she remarked, 'for we are poor now and cannot afford to give dinners', while Kitty wrote pathetically from Stratfield Saye to call to mind the previous year when they had all dined together but 'now I am alone, and most anxious, while [he] is probably with you'. She hardly impinged on the life which her husband had made for himself with Harriet and Charles. The 'trio' had become the centre of his, and their, existence and so it remained for the rest of Harriet's life.

7 The Go-between

Charles's main political career really began when he was appointed in April 1809 to be Joint Secretary of the Treasury, alongside William Huskisson as his colleague. He again succeeded his friend Henry Wellesley, whom he had followed as Chargé des Affaires at Stockholm in 1795 and who now resigned for personal reasons, his wife Lady Charlotte having deserted him for Lord Paget. Charles also succeeded Wellesley as Member of Parliament for Eye, a seat usually kept for a member of the government, as his new office required attendance in the House of Commons.

The two Secretaries to the Treasury occupied crucial posts in the second rank of ministers, being responsible between them for the modern duties of government chief whip, patronage secretary, and the arrangement of business in the House of Commons, as well as the management of the newspaper press and of parliamentary elections, and all the financial affairs of the Treasury which provided the bulk of business in the House of Commons. In the House their duties were crucial to the success of governments. The ties of party in politics had not yet been tightened by commitment to political programmes or even principles. General elections were not fought on national issues which bound members and candidates to government or opposition. MPs were individuals, with varying degrees of independence and their support for measures or ministers was secured by attention to their personal interests, which might involve the distribution of patronage to themselves, their friends, or their important connections and constituents. The scale of the operation was vast: there were 2,000 appointments in the customs service alone, all in the gift of the Treasury where the administration of patronage was concentrated. In the government service, the army and the Established Church appointments were often determined by political considerations, for the days of a professional and politically neutral civil service were far in the future. Wealthy and influential people expected a share in this 'spoils system' and their desires and requests passed through the office of the Secretaries to the Treasury. The Secretary who specialized in this aspect of the department's business thus needed a close knowledge of the interests, motivations and characters of a wide range of men in political life. This involved a great deal of tiresome correspondence and a degree of diplomatic skill: it was a post which few men had the patience or endurance to sustain for long. The Secretaryship was therefore seen either as a stepping-stone on the path of a rising young politician, where he could prove his abilities, or as a suitable destination for the diligent second-rater who could not expect to rise to the highest levels in government.

Charles came to the office at the age of forty-two, no longer a promising young man even though it was a new beginning in his career, and therefore much more in the second category. It was not, however, an obscure situation in the bowels of Whitehall. It placed him in a close and confidential relationship with the Prime Minister who, as head of the Treasury in substance as well as in name, held the ultimate authority in all these matters and also needed to be kept in close touch with parliamentary opinion. He would also on occasion speak for the Prime Minister in the House of Commons. Charles's task was thus not only one of management. He was a go-between in the intricate political relationships of government and Parliament and of outside interests. In essence, he was the Prime Minister's confidential secretary and right-hand man. He had to be a walking political encyclopaedia as well as a labourer at the political treadmill. 'Trusted and confided in by all the leading members of the government, privy to all their secrets, acting as a *liaison* between the party leaders and the rank and file in the House of Commons, managing the government press, and smoothing away difficulties', as the editor of his correspondence has written, 'Arbuthnot played a considerable part in politics behind the scenes.' 'No individual', said Wellington in 1823, 'ever rendered any Government such services as he has to this for a period of now little less than fifteen years.'

At first Charles and Huskisson, with whom he soon became friendly, seem to have shared the varied duties of the secretaryship more or less indiscriminately, though Huskisson's greater financial talents and experience were particularly appropriate to the technical financial side of the work, and Charles, like Wellesley before him, tended to get the larger share of the political management. After only six months, however, Huskisson resigned, following his close friend Canning's departure from the government, and was replaced by Richard Wharton, a political lightweight. From this time the duties of the two Secretaries seem to have been more formally divided, with Charles retaining responsibility for political matters and Wharton for financial, though the division was never complete nor very sharp.

Charles was always conscientious but his natural tendency to worry, to fuss about details and to overwork himself led to criticism of his effectiveness. Huskisson had been a particularly able predecessor, and became one of the few Secretaries to the Treasury in this period to progress successfully to higher office in the Cabinet. He had, wrote one contemporary at the time of his resignation, 'a knowledge of the state of the House of Commons, and the leanings, connections and opinions of everyone in it superior to what I believe any one else possesses'. He was a hard man to follow, and Charles inherited his office at a particularly difficult time for the government which he served. Quite apart from its weakness in the field of war and policy – 1809 was one of the low points in Britain's long struggle against France, and the victories of Wellington in Spain lay unperceived in the distant future, by the political time-scale – it suffered from the effects of internal dissension. It was the year in which Castlereagh and Canning, two of the most important and able of its members, fought a duel over Castlereagh's resentment at the intrigues which he believed Canning was conducting to discredit him and force him out of office. The aged Duke of Portland, who had been appointed Prime Minister in 1807, was too feeble and ill to exercise firm control over his colleagues, and he resigned, following a stroke, at the beginning of September. After some jostling for position, Spencer Perceval, the third of the able disciples of Pitt after Castlereagh and Canning, was appointed – 'the unknown Prime Minister', as he was unkindly, and unjustly, nicknamed by a later commentator.

Perceval was a man of Charles's type. Solid, industrious, reliable and capable rather than brilliant, a devoted family man, with deep religious convictions and spotless private reputation for integrity, he appealed to Charles's similar temperament. He pledged his loyalty to the new Prime Minister in January, 1810: 'Your treatment of me has given you a claim to my most zealous assistance. I only wish that for your sake, the assistance was more valuable; but you shall have the best that I can give.' Ever the conciliator, Charles had hoped at first for the formation of an 'extended administration' – a coalition of parties to include the main opposition group of Grey–Grenville Whigs as well as the personal followers of Lord Sidmouth – but this was impracticable when the government's obvious weakness offered the temptation of greater things to its opponents. It was also the last year of George III's personal monarchy. The old King's mental condition was again giving rise to concern and in 1810 his final relapse into insanity brought the Prince of Wales to the Regency. Grey and Grenville hoped that the Prince's old attachment to the Whigs under Charles James Fox would pay a dividend by bringing them to power: it was not until almost two years later, in June 1812, that their hopes were finally dashed and the Prince resolved to keep his father's ministers.

Spencer Perceval, Prime Minister 1809–12: G.F. Joseph, 1812

All in all, the first three years of Charles's office at the Treasury were years of uncertainty and political instability. Office-seekers and place-hunters were careful not to commit themselves to a losing side, and as long as the government's tenure was shaky they would tend to hold aloof. Mustering a majority in the Commons division lobby was a tricky business, and especially so if a major issue seemed likely to precipitate a crisis. The first major test came with the debate on the Address, opening the new parliamentary session in January 1810. Surprisingly, the government had a majority of nearly 100 – 263 to 167 – but within a few days it was defeated by 195 to 186 on an opposition motion for an enquiry into the failed military expedition to Walcheren, which had precipitated the Castlereagh–Canning duel. Many normal government supporters voted with the opposition, and there followed three successive defeats on financial business – making four defeats in the first week of the session. Matters went from bad to worse when the government tried to muzzle a journalist named Gale Jones whose articles had accused it of mismanagement and corruption. Sir Francis Burdett, defending Jones on the grounds of freedom of speech, was in turn committed to the Tower of London while London raged in fury and armed rebellion almost broke out. Only the resignation of Lord Chatham, the minister responsible for the War Office, and Burdett's moderation on his release from the Tower at the end of the session restored public tranquillity.

The first session of Charles's office at the Treasury had tested his abilities to the full. His task was not helped by the lack of effective speakers on the government front bench, in the absence of Canning and Huskisson particularly. Ryder, the Home Secretary, was nervous, Palmerston, beginning his career at the War Office, was inexperienced and more devoted to pleasure than to parliamentary speaking, and the burden fell on Charles, together with a few others of the second eleven, who were lacking in debating skills and in political weight. Charles's energies in any case were fully occupied in keeping the fragile majority together and trying to handle a vigorous and recalcitrant press who were taking advantage of the government's seeming capacity for self-destruction. He was suffering, he told the Prime Minister, from 'nervous headaches' and other 'disagreeable symptoms' which reduced his effectiveness. The problem was that ministerial supporters were not strictly disciplined, and tended to drift away to their dinners rather than stay to vote. Viscount Lowther told his father in the spring of 1810 that 'Arbuthnot is perfectly *useless*; he is not acquainted with one-third of the House and sits perfectly idle', although he admitted that Lord Chatham was so generally despised that no one could have saved him. Nevertheless, Charles did commit blunders: he annoyed Canning by mistakenly sending him an attendance circular, reserved for the lesser back-bench supporters of government, and by failing to keep confidential matters to himself but discussing them with all and sundry because of his uncertainty. On one occasion he contrived to be too late for a division so that the government's chief whip failed to record a vote. In speaking in the House he limited himself to Treasury matters and lacked the confidence to take part in general debates, even when his senior colleagues were absent. His parliamentary performance was never very impressive, which was to count against him later in life when he failed to achieve Cabinet office under Wellington in 1828 precisely because he could not speak or debate effectively.

Nevertheless, Charles remained a devoted and conscientious servant of the Tory government which lasted, under Perceval and then Liverpool, until 1827. In addition to his parliamentary duties, he was responsible for the management of the newspaper press in order to present a favourable impression to the general public. Since the time of the American and French Revolutions in the later eighteenth century, the people 'out of doors' had played an increasing part in political life, and through the rapidly growing newspaper press had achieved a higher degree of political sophistication and awareness. The management of the press, like the management of the Commons, required constant attention and diplomacy. The British press was insistent on its freedom to report and comment on political affairs and increasing sales and circulations meant that a popular journal could be profitable without having to seek subsidies or bribes from governments. As opposition criticism was always more exciting than support of the status quo, governments were hard put to it to win a favourable hearing. Only in times of crisis and fear of revolution did the propertied class band together to protect the established order. After the threats of domestic subversion and foreign invasion were lifted in the first decade of the nineteenth century, the radical press found an increasing audience among the articulate public, while a series of royal and political scandals after 1806 fed the appetite for agitation and reform. The scandalous life of the Prince Regent was a particular target for journalists and caricaturists, bringing the monarchy itself under public scrutiny and criticism. The work of the government's press manager was not only to present the government's side of every question to a critical public, but to counter radical and opposition propaganda designed to discredit it.

Charles assumed this responsibility at a low point in the government's standing with public opinion. He spent much of his energy in trying to defend the government's, and the Prince's, reputation in the press, and all on a very tight and limited budget. No government had the funds to buy a newspaper outright or even to subsidize it completely. Editors had to be cajoled, persuaded, sometimes threatened, into inserting favourable 'paragraphs', and such paragraphs had to be written and circulated to those likely to accept them. From his first appointment Charles urged his colleagues to provide favourable items from their various departments, and himself undertook what he called the 'irksome' task of dealing with editors – often discreetly, to avoid disclosure of these activities. In 1812, for example, he was 'discreetly active' on behalf of the Prince Regent to combat a press campaign being waged by his estranged wife and her friends in the opposition, and discussed the possibility of helping to set up a new Sunday newspaper called the *Anti-Gallican Monitor* under the editorship of one Lewis Goldsmith. Sums of £1,200 per annum were given to him in 1811 and 1812, but Charles disliked the tone of the paper and reduced the subsidy in 1813. What he called 'that infernal paper' *The Times*, under the John Walter dynasty, was often a thorn in the government's flesh and in 1817 Charles helped a Dr Stoddart, known by his pseudonym as 'Dr Slop' to start up the *New Times* as a rival – though it folded up in 1826. It provided, together with the pro-government *Courier*, a vehicle for propaganda against Queen Caroline in 1820. Charles sent copies round to provincial editors with articles marked in red for republication in the country. In 1809 he was also called upon by Perceval to restrain the ministerial papers from attacking Canning, and he sent for their editors and remonstrated with them – Canning believed the attacks were in fact inspired by Charles, but he emphatically denied it. It was a shady world, nevertheless, in which old established methods which verged, at least, on bribery and corruption were not unknown, but it was a necessary part of the art of political management, whose success or failure it was rarely possible to judge.

In 1812 another political crisis hit the government when Spencer Perceval was assassinated on 11 May in the lobby of the House of Commons. Charles was 'quite overwhelmed' by the news, and was one of the leading mourners at the funeral. He quickly transferred his allegiance to Liverpool, the former Lord Hawkesbury who had advanced his career by appointing him Under-Secretary at the Foreign Office in 1803 and nominating him for the Constantinople embassy. Charles was in any case predisposed to support the Prince Regent's choice of Prime Minister. There had been long negotiations in which it was suggested that Marquess Wellesley, Wellington's elder brother, together with Canning, might be given the task of forming a government, and although Charles declared that he did not wish to serve under Wellesley he still favoured, as in 1809, the possibility of broadening the base of the administration and weakening the Whig opposition – if only to make his task of delivering majorities in the Commons easier. He wrote that he had 'sent to every part of England to get a full attendance' in the House when the negotiations were proceeding. In fact such an arrangement might, if achieved, have altered the direction of Charles's career once again, as it was suggested that he might go to Dublin as Chief Secretary in Ireland, the right-hand man of the Lord Lieutenant. This, Charles wrote to the Prince's private secretary, 'would certainly please me'. Liverpool's appointment left him, however, at the Treasury, where he devoted the next few weeks to trying to arrange for Canning to return to the government in order to strengthen the debating team. He tended, however, as in other matters, to overcomplicate his efforts by bringing in other people to help his schemes, in this case by writing to Huskisson to try to conciliate Canning, only to raise doubts in the latter's mind and lead him to refuse. Canning attributed the breakdown to Charles's meddling: 'Nothing can be kinder than Arbuthnot's intentions' he wrote, 'but I am afraid he bothers things by cross communications.' Lady Bessborough, who patronizingly referred to him as 'little Arbuthnot', when he came to see her with 'a pocketful of notes' as a channel to Canning's friends, observed that he was 'in despair' at the dashing of his hopes, and Charles told Huskisson that 'I am more heartbroken than I can express.' The new government did not inspire confidence. 'We may have victories without end', Charles wrote, 'but they will not improve our Treasury Bench speakers.'

The Prince of Wales's assumption of the Regency was followed by a general election, in which it was Charles's task to secure the new government a sound majority. Again he was accused of failure. He believed that the result was a 'triumph' for the new government and that the Parliament was 'a good one', but others disagreed. '*Entre nous*', wrote Henry Goulburn to Peel, 'it has been most infamously mismanaged, and there have been no candidates found for places the most devoted to our interests, which are consequently now filled by opposition men', and Liverpool's half-brother alleged that he was 'most grossly inattentive to everybody and has given offence to some of your best friends'. Criticism pursued him after his marriage to Harriet and their visit to Paris in 1815: Lowther complained that his six month absence 'caused a sad want of attention and little civilities to the friends of government who now purposely absent themselves, when most wanted'. His worst failure came in March 1816, when the government was defeated in the Commons on a major issue. In a revolt by the back-bench country gentlemen who normally supported government, the House rejected the proposal to continue the wartime income tax (known then as the property tax) in time of peace. The defeat was sprung as a surprise on the government, especially as Charles had assured the Premier that he would have a majority of forty. He also found the House difficult to manage in 1818 over attempts to make provision for the marriages of the Regent's unpopular brothers, the death of Princess Charlotte, his only legitimate offspring, in 1817 having brought the succession to the throne into some danger.

Altogether Charles's experience as manager of the government's majority in the House of Commons was not happy, and in 1819 he complained bitterly about his tribulations:

> Those who stayed, [for a division] complained, as I have heard, that I don't keep good Houses – those who went away equally complain that I require attendance needlessly.

He was

> worn out with bodily fatigue and vexation . . . that our office men would not attend, and that the independent members . . . would not try to support those in office who would not take the trouble of trying to support themselves.

He told the Prime Minister bluntly that unless junior office-holders were hauled over the coals and made to improve their attendance the government would not last longer than another fortnight, and he told Castlereagh that 'the odiousness of my House of Commons duties is become so hateful to me that were I but tolerably independent in my circumstances I would not hold my present office one session longer'. In the easiest times, he wrote, his office required 'the buoyancy of youthful spirits' which he no longer possessed:

> I may be fuller of my own grievances than may be right, but it does indeed dwell upon my mind and spirits that on account of my still having a heavy debt I dare not be a free agent, and either go out of office altogether, or ask whether, after so many years of hard servitude, I might not look up to some other situation, and be thus liberated from the misery of offending everyone whilst I am slaving to preserve the government from disgrace.

From this time onwards, if not before, Charles's sole desire was to escape the 'slavery' of his parliamentary duties and his performance of them consequently did not improve. John Rickman, one of the Clerks of the House of Commons, wrote in 1819 that Charles was 'in himself quite enough to overset any Administration. Equal in small things as in great, having moved an Irish writ a day too soon, he forgot it for a fortnight, and, I think, has not moved any writ this session without some blunder.' His troubles did not diminish in 1820, when the scandal of Queen Caroline's 'trial' before the House of Lords set the country in a flame and, had the Bill against her not been dropped rather than go to the House of Commons, to Charles's great relief, it is likely that the government would have been destroyed by its rejection. In 1821, Charles told his son, 'there never was such a stormy and laborious session'. The King too was aggrieved by his ministers' failure to get him his divorce in 1820, and though Queen Caroline died shortly after his coronation the relations between him and the Prime Minister remained tense.

Within the Cabinet there were still divisions. Canning had re-entered it in 1816 in the rather junior post of President of the India Board, but he hankered after Castlereagh's office of Foreign Secretary and his position as Leader of the Commons. In 1821, however, Canning resigned, feeling his position to be prejudiced by his differences with his colleagues over the Queen's affair. He was believed to have been one of her lovers in the past, and the King was further displeased by a recent speech in which he expressed sympathy and affection for her. His departure further weakened a Cabinet composed largely of lightweights and nonentities. Liverpool wanted him back, and to strengthen his team by also bringing Peel into the Cabinet, while Charles also suggested that efforts should be made to recruit some of the leading Whigs with their followers to bump up the government's majority in the Commons. After several weeks of confused negotiations the plan collapsed, Canning prepared to accept the East India Company's offer to appoint him Governor General, and the Cabinet stumbled on.

The King remained sore with his Ministers throughout the following year. He abused Liverpool for three hours in an audience with Wellesley Pole, Wellington's elder brother and a member of the Cabinet, who unwisely repeated the King's remarks to the Prime Minister. Liverpool, according to Harriet, angrily 'declared that he was weary of office & of serving such a master' and that he would resign as soon as the pressure of business allowed. Harriet thought Pole guilty of 'folly' in telling Liverpool, 'for that the King was such a blockhead nobody minded what he said' and she called in the duke to tell him off for advising his brother to do so. Wellington agreed that 'no men with the feelings of gentlemen' could submit to being talked of in that way by the King, but thought Liverpool had the right to know what was said about him. The storm blew itself out, with Charles acting as usual the emollient role in persuading Liverpool to let the matter drop. Wellington dismissed the King's action as a mere tantrum, saying he liked 'to talk grandly' to make people think that the Prime Minister was merely 'a sort of *maitre d'hotel*' whom he might dismiss at his pleasure, but that it would come to nothing.

One of the causes of the King's displeasure with his ministers was their, and their wives', refusal to invite the royal mistress, Lady

Robert, 2nd Earl of Liverpool: Lawrence, 1804

Conyngham, with whom he was besotted, to their parties – 'one can hardly conceive anything so vulgar' Harriet remarked. Again Charles did his best to smooth things over by talking to Castlereagh – whose wife was one of the chief offenders. They also discussed the possibility of changes in the government to accommodate Peel and Canning, and Castlereagh did his best to reassure Liverpool of the support of his colleagues. In all these discussions Charles did his utmost to soothe ruffled feelings and keep harmony among his colleagues, but the King did not make his task easy by provoking Liverpool, in particular, with further demands. He next proposed to give a canonry at Windsor to a Mr Sumner, whose only recommendation was that he had been tutor to Lady Conyngham's son. Liverpool was furious at this royal interference with ecclesiastical patronage and again it was Charles who mediated. The King sent his private secretary Sir Benjamin Bloomfield to insist on Sumner's appointment, and Bloomfield went straight to Charles, to be told that Liverpool was so angry that he was determined to resign if the King did not yield, and to demand an explanation in Parliament. This, as Harriet wrote, 'frightened' Bloomfield who rushed back to Brighton to persuade his royal master to give way. She was disgusted at the 'everlasting bickering & contention' which 'makes office so odious', and scandalized at the King's 'wanting to prostitute the high dignities in the Church in order to gratify his absurd passion for Ly Conyngham'. Liverpool then travelled to Brighton to have it out with the King and forced him to give way.

Madame Lieven thought that Lady Conyngham was behind all the King's dissatisfaction with his government. Wellington also went to see the King at the end of May to remonstrate with him over his treatment of his ministers, and reduced his sovereign to sitting in silence and grinding his teeth. Four months later Bloomfield again used Charles as a go-between to persuade Liverpool to make up the quarrel and, after a fashion, it was done. It was no wonder that Castlereagh (now Marquess of Londonderry, after his father's recent death) should say to Harriet 'he wondered Mr Arbuthnot was still alive, he had so much to do, but that they shd not be able to go on without him'.

The government's troubles were not only internal. In the autumn of 1821 Ireland seemed about to lapse into anarchy, with civil disturbances all over the west of the country. It was decided to recall the Lord Lieutenant and Chief Secretary and suggested that Wellington should be sent over as supreme military as well as civil commander. Charles immediately offered to go with him as Chief Secretary, being 'completely sick of the Treasury', but wiser counsels prevailed and it was decided to send a civilian viceroy to avoid the appearance of attempting to subdue Ireland by the sword. Harriet was immensely relieved: 'Ireland would be banishment to me', she confessed, even though she would do anything to relieve Charles of his misery in London. 'He is much too good for me', she had confided to her journal in March: 'I feel I do not deserve anything so perfect. There never existed anyone half so amiable or so good as he is.'

As the parliamentary session again approached in February 1822, Charles's tribulations in the House of Commons returned. He told Harriet after the first debate that 'there was a very unpleasant temper in the House', with a rebellious spirit among the government's back-benchers who wanted reductions in taxes, and the opposition was exploiting the situation by moving for retrenchment and economy. The motion was defeated by a satisfactory majority of 108, but the very elaborate and expensive preparations for the coronation in July 1821 had sounded a jarring note in the midst of the country's economic distress. In March the government suffered a defeat in the Commons on a minor division, and scraped home by only four votes on an opposition motion to repeal the salt tax, which if carried would have destroyed their financial policy and forced them to resign. This close shave encouraged the opposition still further, and in early May they beat the ministry by fifteen on a motion to suppress one of the offices of postmaster-general, as part of their campaign to reduce expenditure and also diminish the patronage influence of government. Harriet wrote that the country gentlemen who normally supported government had 'behaved shamefully': 'We are at daggers drawn', she declared.

The Cabinet resolved to crack the whip, and a warning was sent out to the government's supporters that if they were beaten again the ministers would resign. The tactic was effective and when the civil list was voted the government's majority returned to over 100. They were almost immediately thrown into turmoil again by Castlereagh's death, and although this solved some of their problems by precipitating the reconstruction of the Cabinet and the admission of Canning as Foreign Secretary, it heralded the end of Charles's career at the Treasury. Not only did it give him the opportunity to change his office but it also induced Harriet to insist that he give up the role he had filled in close collaboration with Castlereagh because of her horror of his successor. Charles approved of Canning's return to office, as he had of Peel's earlier appointment to the Home Office, as it strengthened the government front bench, and Canning was a far more brilliant speaker than Castlereagh had been. Politically, however, the reconstruction of the Cabinet in 1822 marked the beginning of the 'Liberal Tory' period of Liverpool's administration, with the retirement of die-hards like Sidmouth and the admission of younger men with more liberal views.

Charles and Harriet failed to move with the 'new Toryism'. Their

regrets concerning Castlereagh's death influenced them to resist any
change in the policies and principles they associated with his memory.
Charles's attitude, whether due to Harriet's influence or not, was
becoming more and more conservative. He had earlier supported
Catholic emancipation – always a favourite measure of Canning's, and
one on which individual members of the government were free to vote
according to personal conviction, but in the twenties he became
unsympathetic. Harriet was furiously anti-Canningite, more for personal
than political reasons, and urged Charles to give up his post at the
Treasury which obliged him to work closely with him as Leader of the
Commons. She believed that Canning 'has no moral principle in public
affairs' and looked only to personal advantage, not public good. She
considered him 'a tricking, dishonest politician' and when he resigned
in 1821 wrote that she was 'quite sure we sh^d do a great deal better
without him'. Charles disagreed with her and told her that she was
'very indiscreet & judged exceedingly ill upon this point; but, however,
I did not change my opinion.' In 1821 she asserted that Canning was 'in
every way an improper person' to be Governor-General of India; such a
man ought to be 'a man of high rank in order to gratify the inordinate
love of *grandeur* of the English residents, and a man of high honour &
of strict & impartial justice to promote the comfort & happiness of the
Hindoos. I would not trust Mr Canning in so responsible a situation.'
When Canning was sworn in to the Foreign Secretaryship she wrote
that it was 'most painful to me' that 'the places of my dear lamented
friend are to be filled by one who was always his *ungentlemanlike*
opponent.' Castlereagh's widow and friends, according to Harriet, also
deplored Canning's succession though she admitted that from beyond
the grave Castlereagh might approve of it – but then he 'had an angelic
temper & was incapable of bearing malice against any one', even
one who 'had endeavoured to undermine him with the meanest
hypocrisy. . . . I cannot now see without feelings of the utmost
bitterness his place so unworthily filled. It makes me more than ever
anxious that Mr A. sh^d leave the office he now holds & which brings
him into such personal contact with the leader of the H. of Commons.'

Harriet's urging that Charles should change his post came at a time
when he was himself weary of the laborious and thankless tasks in
which he had spent so many years. He told Liverpool that his health
was beginning to break down because of the arduous duties and long
hours, often being detained at the House till two or three in the
morning; to his friend and colleague Lord Bathurst he added that,
'Independently of being worn out by long drudgery . . . it would have
been strange for me to have retained the management of the House of
Commons, when I assure you that last year I made my continuance a

sort of favour to my much loved friend'. The truth was that Harriet could not bear to stay in their Downing Street house now that Castlereagh was gone, and she could not bear the thought of Charles serving his successor, whoever it might have been.

Nevertheless, Charles could not afford to retire completely. His financial affairs were now reaching a crisis. The farm at Woodford was not profitable, and Harriet's schemes for improving it as a country residence cost money. Charles's sons and daughters were launching into the world and needed his help. He could look forward to a substantial inheritance from Mrs Lisle, his first wife's mother, but she might not die for some years. Charles therefore still needed an official salary, and he grasped the opportunity for an exchange of offices in January 1823 when Huskisson was promoted to the Presidency of the Board of Trade from his post as First Commissioner of Woods and Forests. Charles was nominated as his successor and took up his new duties with relief at his release from what he called his 'interminable slavery'.

Charles's tenure of the Secretaryship to the Treasury was one of mixed fortunes. His failings in the management of the Commons were more obvious to the observer than his successes in the more private and confidential role he occupied 'behind the scenes'. Looking back on his career as patronage secretary, he observed that during eleven years Liverpool 'never made any appointment, great or small, without first talking it over with me' and it is clear that he performed a vital role in this taxing and, in early nineteenth-century politics, essential sphere. It was one always open to criticism from those who were disappointed in their hopes of advancement or simply dissatisfied with the government's general performance, and Charles felt that criticism keenly. He never took kindly to what he considered unfair disparagement, and was always inclined to resent the impression that he was not valued at his true worth by his colleagues or the political world in general. In fact he was generally respected for his honesty and integrity, if not for great talents, by political opponents as well as by friends. Despite his access to the whole range of government patronage, he never used his influence with Liverpool to provide anything for himself or his family. In his later years he wrote:

> With the exception of recommending for preferment a brother in the church, and asking for a clerkship in the Treasury for a nephew, I never endeavoured, nor ever did obtain, one single favour for myself or for my family during the many years that the whole patronage of the Treasury . . . passed, as I may truly say, through my hands. I have at least the consolation of knowing that I did not grasp at favours when I might have had them, and that I never betrayed the unlimited confidence which was placed in me.

It was not an unworthy record in an age when favouritism and corruption were still part of the political scene, though both governments and public opinion were turning against them and their prevalence was rapidly diminishing. Charles played a minor but significant role in the progress towards a less cynical political system.

Charles's role in Liverpool's administration had always been more than that of mere patronage secretary and chief whip. His most valuable service lay in his activity as a go-between, confidential adviser, and eyes and ears for the Prime Minister. Harriet wrote of his 'most essential services' to the King, Prime Minister, and Castlereagh as Leader of the Commons: 'for many years [he] has executed the duties of a most arduous & unpleasant office in a manner satisfactory to every one'.

Charles's retirement from the Treasury was not the end of his political career but it opened another stage, taking him away from the hurly-burly of late nights and incessant business to a less burdensome and less prominent role, if one not lacking in importance. It also signalled a change in the balance of his activities between public duties and private concerns. For the remainder of their lives, these were for Charles and Harriet closely bound up with their most intimate friend, the Duke of Wellington.

8 Personalities and Politics

Charles and Harriet continued to live near the centre of political life after 1823 mainly because of their connection with Wellington and Charles's continued activity as a political conciliator in the sometimes stormy atmosphere of Liverpool's later Cabinets. Though Charles was happy to give up what he called 'my long drudgery' in the House of Commons, he hoped and even expected that Liverpool would continue to consult and confide in him. He thought that Liverpool

> seemed very anxious that I should continue to be his confidential friend. At his time of life it might not be pleasant to part with an old channel of intercourse and communication, and I shall do my utmost to be of all the use to him in my power.

He even proposed that his successor should be Stephen Lushington on the grounds that

> if I am to be in confidential intercourse with Ld. Liverpool, . . . we can satisfy him with whatever share of confidence we may think fit to place in him. . . . Be it always remembered that his replacing of me would be in some respects merely nominal. He wd have to drudge in the H. of Cs & to give *bad dinners*; but he never wd be admitted into confidence either by Liverpool or Canning, & I with a mind & Body more at ease shd be ready & able to lend to both of them all the *confidential aid* in my power.

Charles evidently had no doubt that Liverpool would wish to continue to treat him as his confidential adviser, while leaving his successor to perform the merely routine duties of Secretary to the Treasury and relieve Charles of the stress and labour which he found so distasteful.

The cup was almost dashed from his lips however when the proposed new arrangements were thrown into disarray by the refusal of Wallace, the Vice-President of the Board of Trade, to serve under Huskisson, whose move to the Presidency of the Board had opened up his former post for Charles. Wallace demanded the Woods and Forests for himself, and Canning and Liverpool felt it necessary to agree to avert a crisis. Liverpool suggested that as a temporary measure Charles should share the Presidency of the Board of Trade with Huskisson until a better office could be found for Wallace, but Charles was convinced that everyone would consider him as merely Huskisson's assistant and not his equal, particularly as Huskisson was much more likely to shine in the House of Commons. He poured out his injured feelings to Huskisson, writing indignantly that it was 'a blow that has struck me to the ground & has left me with no other wish than to pass the remainder of my days away from the annoyances of public life. . . . Never were my feelings so cut to pieces.' Liverpool 'could have commanded my life almost – my best days have been devoted to him' – and this was his reward. Harriet stiffened his resolution. She suspected that Liverpool and Canning 'wd get him between them and work upon his good nature till he agreed', and she and Wellington urged Charles not to go up to town until the matter was settled. Charles 'was in such a state of agitation & indignation at such treatment' that the duke joined in and wrote to urge Liverpool to give way, and Charles followed up with a letter of his own. He pointed out that he had originally consented to become Secretary to the Treasury after serving in the higher rank of an ambassador, simply as a means 'of endeavouring to be useful' and because he was

> averse to the notion of retiring upon a pension in the prime of life. . . . No one . . . but myself can tell how trying at times my duties have been, & when my mind has been almost ready to break with vexation I have comforted myself with feeling that to you I had devoted my best & most strenuous exertions.

Huskisson and Canning evidently felt that he was being difficult, but Liverpool was touched by Charles's anguish and gave way, writing that he would never wish him to do anything which he felt to be derogatory to his character merely to accommodate him. The appointment to the Woods and Forests was therefore confirmed and Wallace was given the post of Master of the Mint. 'This made us very happy,' Harriet concluded.

Charles accordingly remained, at least for the time being, in close touch with the inner secrets of government, and corresponded with Liverpool and Huskisson, who was an old and close friend from many years ago, on confidential matters of policy and appointments. He was also still closely in touch with Wellington, both through Harriet and also, as he considered himself, as the duke's political agent and protector of his interests when Liverpool seemed to be falling under the influence of Canning, or losing the confidence of George IV.

The King's relations with his Prime Minister continued to be abrasive after 1822. He had never forgiven Liverpool for the failure to get his divorce two years earlier, and after Castlereagh's death he objected strongly to Liverpool's suggestion that Canning should succeed him, being still sore at Canning's attitude towards the late Queen. Charles used all his tact and diplomacy to bring the King and Prime Minister into closer accord. When George called him to Windsor to discuss his plans for new building improvements there, they took the opportunity to talk about the state of the government, and Charles passed on the information about the King's feelings to Liverpool, 'my object being', as he wrote, 'to do you all the good in my power'. He warned Liverpool about the malign influence of Sir William Knighton, the King's new private secretary, 'the greatest rogue in England' according to Harriet, who wanted to be made a privy councillor and resented Liverpool's refusal to make him one. 'It is right you should know that as long as his mind shall continue to writhe under mortification and disappointment the, you must expect all the disservice & all the injury that he can inflict', Charles wrote. Though the King himself was at present 'actuated by no angry feelings', he too was apprehensive about the prospect of Canning's entry into the Cabinet, believing that Liverpool, who was becoming more lethargic since the death of his wife in 1821, would be dominated by him. As Wellington remarked, however, George disliked Liverpool and wanted to get rid of him: Charles believed that the King would rather replace him with Canning than continue having him as Prime Minister under Canning's control. He observed that the King thought that Canning would pay him more 'personal attention' than Liverpool did, and would not obstruct 'his personal objects in buildings, purchases, &c.' as Liverpool was inclined to do for reasons of public economy. He ended his warning with the assurance that Wellington would support Liverpool and his government 'with *his very heart's blood*', and that he (Charles) had told the King so: both the King and the duke wanted Liverpool to assert himself and be the 'real Minister' and not a tool of Canning's. Charles added his plea to theirs: all would be well if Liverpool would act decisively himself and not appear to allow Canning to seem to be his sole adviser.

Liverpool's response was indignant. 'The K. is mistaken if he supposes that I have any anxious desire to remain in his service', he wrote. 'He cannot be too strongly apprized of this truth.' It was for Liverpool himself to decide whether to go on or retire, 'but let the K. take care that he does not make the close of a reign which has been hitherto most glorious, & upon the whole most prosperous, stormy & miserable'. He was nevertheless grateful for Charles's warning, and the improvement in the relations between George IV and his ministers which followed owed a good deal to Charles's skill at oiling the wheels.

He also acted as intermediary between Liverpool and Wellington, noting in a letter to his friend Lord Bathurst that the Prime Minister was anxious to keep friendly relations with Wellington and assuring him that he would do all in his power to keep Wellington in harmony with Liverpool. He also urged Bathurst to speak out in Cabinet to support the duke when he agreed with his opinions, believing that Wellington felt lonely and isolated in the ministry. He also had confidential conversations with Peel, who was suspicious and resentful of Canning's influence, hoping to enlist him in the anti-Canning faction.

Politically, at this period of their lives Charles and Harriet were dominated by their dislike of Canning. Harriet's feelings were the most extreme, and owed much to her previous hero-worship of Castlereagh, but they were strengthened by her hatred of Canning's liberal attitude in foreign affairs and on the Catholic question, and by her conviction – in which she was not alone, but joined by Lord Grey, for one – that he was an untrustworthy politician whose love of power was greater than the principles he professed. After 1822 her journal is full of criticism and condemnation of Canning's foreign policy, his dictatorial attitude towards his colleagues, and his alleged errors and ill-temper.

In 1824 she discovered the story of Canning's parentage and upbringing – his father had been disinherited for making an unsatisfactory marriage, deserted his wife and son, who were found living in 'a wretched garret in Holborn', and, after his death, Canning's mother went on the stage and became 'the kept mistress of an actor', while her son was sent to Eton and Oxford by his wealthy grandfather. 'To those who, like me, think there is a good deal *in blood*', Harriet declared, 'it may appear that Mr Canning's want of principle or high & honourable feeling may be derived from the stock he sprung from.'

Charles was less sweeping in his condemnation. He had been a friend of Canning's in their early days when both were starting on their public careers, and he always conceded that Canning was a man of great talents if he did not always agree with the way they were applied. He had tried in 1812 to reunite Canning with the government to broaden its political base and he continued to hope that this would one day be achieved. As one responsible for keeping up the government's majority in Parliament Charles was very conscious of the need to have Canning's oratorical powers on their side, and Harriet wrote in 1820 that her husband was 'very angry with me' for saying that the government would be better off without him – he called it 'the most gross want of good judgement in me' not to see his value to the front bench, and 'abused and scolded me for being so wrong headed'. It was almost the only occasion after their marriage that they came to the verge of a quarrel: in 1824 she wrote that they used to 'quarrel terribly' when Harriet wanted the duke to resign from the Cabinet over the Spanish colonies and Charles considered it vital for him to stay in to keep Canning under control. Wellington on both occasions agreed with Charles: both were men of the political world, pragmatic politicians who valued ends above means, while Harriet judged with her emotions

George Canning: Lawrence, c. 1825

and feelings about character. She found it 'most painful' when Canning was sworn in to Castlereagh's old office in 1822, whereas Charles and the duke were relieved that his talents were now to be at the service of the government and a loose cannon tied down at last. George IV too had his regrets at having to accept Canning into his service, and found it difficult to condone his liberal, at times seemingly radical, leanings – Wellington told Harriet in 1824 that he spoke of Canning 'with the deepest abhorrence'.

The last years of Liverpool's administration were in many ways frustrating ones for the Arbuthnots. Canning seemed to monopolize their thoughts to the point of becoming a phobia, while Liverpool's growing infirmity, tiredness and irritable manner seemed to indicate that he was no longer in control and, worse, no longer their friend. Charles and Wellington spent a lot of time fighting the King's prejudice and trying to convince him of his Prime Minister's indispensability, if only to keep Canning out of the premiership. Visiting Brighton in 1824, for example, Charles begged the King to be civil to Liverpool, and the King boasted to Wellington that he had done so – though Harriet noted that Liverpool and Wellington were 'barely civil to each other'. The duke considered that Liverpool was completely dominated by Canning and it took all Charles's tact and diplomacy to keep good relations between them. He had a long talk with Liverpool in March 1824, telling him of Wellington's dissatisfaction with what he considered his lack of influence in the Cabinet, and assuring him that 'these disagreeable feelings wd be done away with if he & Mr Canning wd show more cordiality & confidence' towards the duke. 'I daresay this conversation will have no effect', Harriet reflected, though Liverpool acquiesced in all that Charles said. Six months later she wrote that Liverpool was completely under Canning's influence and that he and Charles had consequently become completely estranged: Liverpool, she asserted, was 'a man entirely without feelings of friendship', and Charles felt it deeply that after serving him faithfully for so many years he should no longer be in his confidence. The duke, as always, gave comforting support, told her that Charles 'was not of a calibre to be considered merely a blind follower of Liverpool', and that Liverpool was completely dominated by Canning at present but that 'the moment Lord L. got into any scrape or difficulty he wd send for Mr A. exactly the same as if he had not treated him with neglect. To all this', she wrote, 'I could answer that Lord Liverpool was an odious person from his total want of feeling.'

The estrangement proved only temporary, and by the end of the year Charles and Liverpool were back on their old terms and Liverpool's 'coolness' had 'quite gone off'. Charles took the opportunity to assure

Liverpool of Wellington's devotion, which pleased him and brought him into a better frame of mind towards the duke. Charles also discussed affairs with other leading members of the Cabinet who all agreed with his view of Wellington and with his dislike of Canning. Charles felt that he had countered Canning's excessive influence in the government, but feared that Harriet's hostility towards Canning would induce the duke to resign, and remove a vital check on Canning's policies – hence the occasion when she and Charles quarrelled 'terribly', as Harriet recorded.

The major difference between Wellington and Canning arose in 1824 over Canning's plan to recognize the independence of Spain's former Latin American colonies, in the belief that this would gain their gratitude and promote Britain's commercial interests there. Wellington and the 'coterie' around George IV however believed that Canning was merely seeking personal fame among European and English liberals by bringing off a great coup and that, in terms of British interests, it was more important to maintain good relations with Spain in Europe. The King hated the idea of recognizing rebels against a legitimate sovereign, and made comparisons between Bolivar, the leader of the rebels, and Daniel O'Connell in Ireland. Charles feared that once again relations between the King and his ministers would reach a crisis. He wrote to Bathurst that Liverpool had lately 'rather abstained from talking with me' on confidential topics, and urged him to support the duke's view that Britain should not recognize any of the new states unless they had a settled and stable *white* government and a revenue sufficient to keep up a necessary military strength. Charles feared that Wellington might resign if he was not supported, which would cut off his and Harriet's main source of political information and influence.

Canning got his way over the independence of the Spanish colonies but Wellington stayed in office, though angry at Canning's policy and tactics, and the storm blew over, only to return shortly afterwards over the Catholic Bill, a proposal to free Roman Catholics from civil penalties, which Canning supported. Liverpool and Peel seemed determined to resign, and Liverpool to advise the King to make Canning Prime Minister. Wellington and Charles did their utmost to avert the disaster, Charles busily running round and talking to people while the Cabinet held a series of stormy meetings. At last this storm too blew over, Canning agreeing not to press the Catholic question and after the House of Lords rejected the Relief Bill Liverpool and Peel decided to stay in office.

Harriet and Charles saw Wellington as the calm centre in all this turbulence. Harriet wrote in 1826, on the eve of the duke's departure on a mission to St Petersburg that he

Vase presented to Harriet by Wellington on his return from St Petersburg, 1826

is so important at home! The connecting link between all the different factions, who all look to him with such implicit confidence, frank, honest, conciliating, the protector of all that are ill-used & the only person that can at all curb Mr Canning & Mr Huskisson in their liberal policy.

In this role he had Charles's assistance, for as even Canning admitted, 'no one had ever had the entire confidence of the Prime Minister to the extent that Mr A. had Lord Liverpool's & that he believed he had always made the most honest & upright use of it.' During the duke's absence in Russia in 1826 Charles even managed a *rapprochement* with Canning, going to talk to him on the state of the country after the financial crash of that year and agreeing with him that Liverpool's policy needed to be modified.

Harriet was pleased that Charles was on better terms with Canning 'for it makes his position in the Government much more agreeable; but,' she could not help adding, 'he must only take great care not to be drawn into any of his dirty jobs.' She suspected that Canning was trying to prolong Wellington's stay in Russia in order to hold a general election in his absence and to favour pro-Catholic candidates. By the time of the election in the summer Harriet was convinced that Canning was 'the entire master' of both the King and Liverpool and that the King's 'sudden fondness for Mr Canning' would cut Wellington out of royal favour. She asserted that the King had allowed Canning to nominate several of his friends for peerages at the dissolution, even though he had to search 'the highways and hedges' for suitable persons. She was beginning to suspect that Canning would be the King's choice as the next Prime Minister. Wellington told her that his old intimacy with the King was now at an end, the King believing that Canning would be 'a much less scrupulous friend'. 'I wish the King joy of his task', she commented, and wrote of 'the disgusting selfishness of the King's character'. After the elections were over fresh contentions broke out in the Cabinet over economic and foreign policies, and she thought 'the whole concern so very disagreeable that I wd give anything to be out of it & to see the Gov^t broken up.'

That is indeed what happened early in the new year. Liverpool suffered a severe stroke on 17 February and was found unconscious on the floor of his breakfast room. Despite what medical attention could do for him, he could hardly speak or move and it was clear that there was little hope for him, though the King and his colleagues agreed to wait for a while to see if there were prospects of recovery before replacing him. Harriet paid tribute to his earlier vigour and success as Prime Minister, and ascribed the difficulties of his later years to 'the declining state of his health & to the tyrannical influence acquired over him by Mr Canning'. She feared that Canning would succeed him, her own choice – naturally the duke – being 'not the *favorite* in the field', the betting in the clubs being on Canning with Lord Lansdowne, a moderate Whig, as second favourite. Wellington had only recently been appointed Commander-in-Chief of the army on the Duke of York's death, and it would not do for a serving soldier to be head of the government. Nevertheless she declared her certainty that, if given the chance, he would be 'the best Minister we ever [had]'. She was not without hope, for she felt sure that if Canning were appointed the right wing of the Tory party, including the duke, Peel, Lord Eldon and several others, would refuse to serve under him, and the country would not bear the opposition. Perhaps the duke would emerge as the compromise candidate. Whatever happened, she and Charles were 'perfectly disinterested' for

> our position in all this is particularly agreeable; our pension out of office is the same as the salary of this office, we sh^d lose nothing but the house, so that we don't care whether we stay or go, & we want nothing of any sort or kind; we wd not change our office for any other in the Kingdom.

She had no hesitation in using the almost royal 'we': she hardly considered that Charles would have a different opinion.

Charles in any case was plunged back into the role he had played so often in the past, to Harriet's pleasure. He was now to be found in confidential discussions with Peel, with Sir William Knighton the King's secretary, whom he put into a good humour by saying that they shared the same objective of giving the country a strong government without any personal interests, and with other leading personalities. Wellington was anxious lest Charles's activity should be interpreted as an intrigue to make him Prime Minister – 'I never saw the Duke so much vexed about any thing in my life', Harriet wrote – but whether or not that was Charles's object, it is at least likely that he was trying to block Canning's appointment.

If so, however, he was unsuccessful. A number of Tory Lords tried to start a bandwagon for the duke, but the King told Wellington himself that his office of Commander-in-Chief ruled him out altogether. Harriet could not entirely conceal her disappointment – 'I am sure it is very disinterested in me wishing the Duke shᵈ be Minister', she wrote, for if he were she would see hardly anything of him and his society was 'the greatest real pleasure of my life'. The King however had made up his mind to have Canning, and was only anxious to have it arranged without a political crisis. A series of meetings between the senior politicians and the King culminated in Canning's formal appointment on 10 April, over seven weeks after Liverpool's stroke, and there followed the immediate resignations of the Tory section of the government, including Wellington, Lords Westmorland and Bathurst, and Peel, 'to the number of near 30' as Harriet recorded. Charles of course was among them.

9 A Royal Partnership

Charles's move to the post of First Commissioner of Woods and Forests in 1823 brought him into an even closer relationship with George IV. Since he had become Secretary to the Treasury in 1809 a significant part of Charles's duties had involved service to George as Prince of Wales and Prince Regent. The Prince's interests were of major concern to the government, particularly since his father's declining health might at almost any time bring him to the throne, and put him in a position to change the ministry if he so wished. Charles therefore set himself to gratify the Prince wherever the duties of his office made it possible. In particular, he sought to use his influence to manipulate the press on George's behalf. No man suffered more from the attentions of a press that, then as now, enjoyed nothing so much as making salacious disclosures about the private lives of royalty. Admittedly George gave the newspapers more material than anyone else to work on, but that did not reduce the harm that the press was thought to be doing to the monarchy in general. Colonel McMahon, the Prince's private secretary, was in frequent communication with Charles about the iniquities of journalists and editors – in 1812 he was 'in a rage at the diabolical Morning Chronicle' over articles about the Prince and Lady Hertford – and in 1813 threats of disclosures in *The News* found Charles using his diplomatic skills on the editor, T.G. Street. 'I do not wish to make professions', Charles wrote to McMahon, 'but I think I may say that when I can really be of use I shall not be found backward in the Regent's cause.' Although, he added,

> My task is no easy one I assure you . . . the Regent very much mistakes me, & I wd fain add very little knows me if he thinks that I would be lukewarm where he is concerned. It would be strange indeed if I were not bound to him by ever the warmest feeling of gratitude & attachment.

He had not attempted to silence Street, 'but I told him that clamour and declamation would be idly kicking against the pricks'. Two years later, after another interview with Street, he assured McMahon, 'I have him now in a very good humour.'

Charles also gratified the Prince by attending to the wishes and ambitions of his friends, especially in the distribution of patronage. He

King George IV as Prince Regent: Lawrence, c. 1819

performed an invaluable service in keeping the Prince on good terms with his ministers. In 1811 he had assured McMahon of 'the deep sense wch his condescending goodness has made upon me. In former days when I had the honour of more frequently seeing his Royal Highness, his treatment of me was invariably most flattering & most gracious, & it will be the effort of my life to merit a continuation of his good opinion.' George remained highly appreciative of Charles's efforts, and in 1822 wrote of 'your kind and affectionate conduct towards me', which was 'not new, because I have always found it to be the case', and he assured him of 'my regard and warm esteem'.

It was indeed Charles's close relationship with the King and the trust he inspired in him that led Liverpool to appoint him to the office of Woods and Forests in 1823. George's extravagance had not abated with the years, and the Prime Minister was anxious that his campaign for public economy should not be undermined by the King's ambitious and highly expensive projects for beautifying the capital and refurbishing the royal palaces, projects which involved the work of the department. Liverpool told Peel that the office had become one of 'peculiar delicacy' because of the close connection between its public responsibilities and the King's private affairs, and that 'for such a situation and relation Arbuthnot is particularly qualified'. If Charles, as a former Treasury minister, was intended by Liverpool to exercise a restraining hand on the King's enthusiasm it cannot be said that he was entirely successful. On the other hand, it brought him into an even closer association with George and it gave him an important role in the development of the fashionable side of London and in particular the layout and ornamentation of the royal parks, which have ever since been the distinctive feature of the area.

Despite its old-fashioned title, Charles's new office was one of some importance. Its major task was to gather and administer the revenues from the Crown lands, which were not granted by Parliament but had long been part of the 'hereditary revenues' of the Crown. In fact, since 1760 the House of Commons had taken these revenues into account in fixing the civil list, the sum which was estimated to be sufficient to maintain the Court, the royal palaces and residences, and to pay the salaries of officers under the Crown, from the Prime Minister to menial servants in the King's household. The Woods and Forests was the department through which the sums from the Crown estates passed, to be applied mainly to their upkeep and development. The Treasury exercised a general oversight of these operations but in practice it was a lax control which allowed the King and the office to have a largely free hand in applying the revenues.

The office's chief responsibility was for the royal parks, roads and estates rather than for buildings, which were the task of the Office of

Works, but the two departments overlapped and worked closely together. Woods and Forests, for example, had charge of the buildings in the royal parks, and the operations of the Office of Works were financed partly from the receipts of the Woods and Forests, as well as from parliamentary grants or the King's Privy Purse. Together, the two departments acted as a kind of ministry of the environment, especially for London where the principal royal lands and buildings were situated.

In the 1820s the government was beginning to concern itself with the improvement as well as the maintenance of the London environment. Great public works and buildings were designed and built to beautify the capital and to provide a grander setting for the centre of the world's greatest empire. The British Museum, the Law Courts, the National Gallery and the newly-formed Trafalgar Square, the Customs House, the Post Office and the new Treasury building in Whitehall and accommodation for other government departments were planned or built during this decade mostly under the supervision of the Office of Works. The King himself, his lifelong obsession with building and refurbishing the royal residences now amounting almost to a mania, undertook the rebuilding of Windsor Castle and Buckingham House, and the completion of the royal highway begun in the Regency and bearing his name, from Regent's Park to Westminster. These projects involved Charles's department. In 1823 the King quarrelled with Colonel Stephenson, the head of the Office of Works, and though Charles exercised his usual emollient role the King remained distrustful of him, and insisted on the appointment of a special commission of eight members to superintend the works at Windsor in 'matters of taste'. Charles and Wellington were among the members. In the mid 1820s the enormous expense of Nash's works at Buckingham Palace attracted public criticism, and although the office of Woods and Forests was not directly responsible, it was accused of failing to exercise adequate financial control. Charles was obliged to defend Nash in the House of Commons against allegations of extravagance and bad taste.

Charles's work in beautifying the parks was his chief contribution to the work of his department. As Harriet later wrote, 'when he took the office there was not a lodge that was not a disgrace to the town, filthy cow sheds & no better.' Hyde Park was still a rural pasture for cows, whose milk was sold on the spot by milkmaids, and apart from the fashionable Rotten Row where the quality rode at weekends it was more like a common than a cultivated park. Charles was responsible for building the lodges at Stanhope and Cumberland Gates and at Hyde Park Corner. He himself chose Decimus Burton as the architect for these projects, having been impressed by his work on the buildings he designed in Regent's Park – 'works which pleased my eye, from their

Grand entrance to Hyde Park by Decimus Burton: from a drawing by Thomas H. Shepherd, 1828

Serpentine Bridge, Hyde Park, by C. Rennie: from a drawing by Thomas H. Shepherd, 1827

architectural beauty and correctness', he wrote. Charles was also responsible for Rennie's bridge at Kensington Gardens, and for opening Birdcage Walk to the public. Altogether he made Hyde Park 'really beautiful', Harriet wrote, and Londoners still owe him their gratitude for taking the crucial steps in the development of the parks as a pleasant and fashionable place of recreation in the middle of the crowded capital city.

He was also called upon to deal with many of the problems involved in the growth of the fashionable West of London. The policing of the royal parks posed questions not unfamiliar in the present age. In 1824 Charles bemoaned to Peel, the Home Secretary, that 'we cannot prevent the mischief wh. daily arises from idle boys', who 'destroy all they can; – & the Park Keepers . . . on their parts think of nothing but their dealings in cows' (which were pastured in the park). He begged Peel to find a more effective policing system. Another problem with a modern tinge was the excessive demand for stabling and accommodation for carriages around Westminster. The office built the 'Parliamentary mews' between Great George Street and the Abbey but Charles soon complained that the number of applications for this accommodation was far greater than could be gratified. Early nineteenth-century London had its parking problem too.

Charles's new department was thus becoming more important in this period. Thirty years before, the Woods and Forests and the Office of Works had been regarded largely as sinecures, but by the 1820s they had become active and busy, if still not very efficient, departments. The Woods and Forests was accommodated in a central position, across the road from the Admiralty in Whitehall and on the corner of Whitehall Place, adjacent to Charles's official residence, and in early nineteenth-century terms it was quite a large department. In 1829 it employed a staff of thirty-four in the London office – a size comparable with that of the Home and Foreign Offices at the same period – besides numerous local inspectors, surveyors and others in the provinces. Charles counted therefore in the second rank of ministers and apart from his official responsibilities he also had the advantage of a close relationship with the King.

There was however one major disadvantage. The office of Woods and Forests was worth considerably less in salary than the Secretaryship to the Treasury and Charles's financial problems reasserted themselves. A drop of £2,000 a year – half his previous income – made his position very precarious and alarmed his friends. He was also still £15,000 in debt from his Constantinople embassy and though he was able to pay the interest while he was at the Treasury it now became impossible to do so. Liverpool, probably at Wellington's instigation, and with the

King's approval, arranged for Harriet to receive a pension of £1,200 p.a. on the civil list, which, since it was in her name, could be paid while Charles was earning an official salary. It was clearly understood that the pension was given in recognition of Charles's services and to help make up their incomes. In addition, towards the end of 1823 and again at Wellington's request, Lord Bathurst, Secretary of State for the Colonies, another friend in the government, offered Charles an additional post in his department as Agent for the colony of Ceylon, which Huskisson had resigned, at £1,200 p.a. (gross, £1,100 net). It was virtually a sinecure office but it could be held, with Parliament's approval, together with an efficient post. Wellington wrote that Charles's services over fifteen years merited such a reward, and that it would 'put him at his ease'. Liverpool endorsed the proposal with the acknowledgement that Charles had 'made a considerable sacrifice of income, which he could by no means afford'. He also approved on the grounds that it would be 'a public advantage that that agency should be given to a man of business, and in a great measure as a reward for other public services'. Huskisson and Canning also signified their agreement in principle, but Huskisson pointed out that in the current climate of public sensitivity on the subject of sinecures, especially offices held by members of the government but executed by deputies, there might be awkward questions in the House of Commons, where the radical MP Joseph Hume was actively campaigning for economy in public expenditure. Huskisson suggested that it would create less comment if the post was given nominally to Charles's eldest son and the salary reduced to £800. Even Hume, Liverpool thought, could not carp at this step in view of Charles's long service and deserving character.

Charles thought otherwise. His first reaction was that the agency was 'not the most desirable species of income', but 'I have never been much of a gainer by public employment & I owe it to my family to take thankfully whatever is offered.' In January 1824 however he told Bathurst that 'without vanity or presumption', the agency could not be thought to be 'exactly suited to my station in public life' and 'it would not do for me to take it if there should be a necessity of lowering it in any way'. He had also discovered that if he later left office and took up his diplomatic pension of £2,000, which was still in abeyance, he could not hold the agency at the same time, so its value was considerably lessened. He therefore declined it altogether, adding that 'I could not assent to be under any obligation to Canning. Circumstances have forced me not to feel very favourably towards him . . . it would be a horror to me to owe obligations to which my mind could make no return.'

By this time, the situation had been resolved in another way. Charles first considered the possibility of reducing his expenses by selling

Woodford, but Harriet considered the valuation of £40,000 too low. She knew how miserable it would make Charles to give up his country estate and his farming hobby.

> Tho' I do not think this place so indispensable to my comfort as it is to yours, [she wrote] still even for myself I shd be very sorry indeed, & I know it wd be so horrible to you that I shd. be really in despair. . . . Pray keep up yr spirits, & do not talk of being broken down, my dearest. I look forward to our passing many happy years together, & if we can but get rid of these money concerns & make the farm pay *tolerably*, our next ten years will be happier than the last.

Harriet's suggestion was to appeal to the King to get him to buy the estate for £45,000 on the understanding that they would buy it back when Mrs Lisle died and Charles inherited her property and fortune. In the meantime, however, George IV had his own idea. Dissipated scoundrel as the King appeared in the public prints, and even in the opinion of his own friends and associates, he possessed a kind heart and a genuine wish to make those around him happy. At the end of November 1823 he wrote to Wellington of his concern that 'our poor friend Arbuthnot's affairs are in a most desperate and wretched state, and without some immediate and most material relief his present situation must not only be abandoned, in all probability, but it would be necessary for him to quit (for a time at least) this country', to avoid his creditors. The King proposed to borrow £15,000 and to make a gift of it, through Wellington, so that Charles could pay off his outstanding debt, and, he added, in a letter to the duke, 'I beg, my dear friend, that in doing this, you will say everything kind and affectionate to Mr and Mrs Arbuthnot, because I know how much you love and regard them.'

The King's unsolicited generosity touched both Charles and Harriet deeply. 'With everything at home to make me happy', Charles wrote to Sir William Knighton,

> I still was a wretched being; and you have turned me into a most happy one. But you have done more than this – you have made happy one of the best of women – one whose strength of mind has supported me under the severest trials, and one who will ever join with me in thanks and gratitude to you. May God bless you.

He also wrote directly to the King in effusive gratitude, and assured him that 'my beloved sovereign has made two beings happy, & that those two beings were even long since devoted to him.' Harriet assured Knighton that 'you have sent Mr Arbuthnot back to me the happiest man in England', and to Charles she declared

> Believe me I rejoice ten times more in the ease & comfort all this will procure to you, than for any advantages to myself. You were always so kind to me & took

John Nash: Lawrence, 1827

such care that *I* at least shd. feel no want of money that I have never wished for a comfort more than I have always had. . . . Dearest love, we shall indeed be rich & happy, but let us be *stingy* in future & take care that such distress shall never come upon us again.

She remained sceptical about the King's consistency;

his first impulses always are kind, but afterwards comes in his selfishness, & by & bye I have no doubt he will say G- d- him, he has ruined me by making me give him £15,000. However that won't signify to us if he only makes the remark to his banker.

However that might be, Charles and Harriet were now able to resume their place in society free from immediate financial worries.

Nevertheless, despite Charles's new found security and his interest in the duties of his new office, within three years he was beginning to dislike his post. This was largely because of his inability to take criticism and his consequent tendency to worry when it came. During the years 1826–28 his department came under fire from the press as well as the Opposition in the House of Commons. There was a good deal of public disquiet about the cost of the royal building programme and the alleged lack of financial control over the extravagance of architects, planners, and builders, as well as controversy over designs and matters of taste. One newspaper attacked 'the extravagant expenditure connected with the Woods and Forests department' and demanded a thorough reform of the office. It alleged that part of its revenues were being applied to other purposes due to the lack of firm financial controls. When he became Prime Minister in 1828 Wellington was also keen to reduce public expenditure and to improve the efficiency of the public offices, and despite his friendship with Charles the Office of Woods and Forests was not excluded from the process of enquiry and reform. It was disclosed that Nash's Regent Street, estimated at first to cost some £385,000, had swallowed up over £1.5 million, and the Serpentine bridge exceeded its estimate of £36,500 by some £9,000. Both these projects were supervised by Charles's department.

In 1828 the Commons appointed a select committee on the Office of Works, whose investigations also touched the Woods and Forests. Though Charles was a member of the committee, as were some other officials, he could not entirely divert its attention and there was much criticism of departmental inefficiency. In 1829 *The Times*, commenting on the triennial report of the Commissioners of Woods and Forests, remarked 'we are amazed at the freedom from salutary control which has been suffered so long to flourish'. When Wellington moved Charles to the Duchy of Lancaster in May 1828 it may well have been part of the duke's efficiency drive, for Lord Lowther, Charles's successor, was pledged to exercise stiffer control over the finances of the department. In 1832 there was a more fundamental reform when the Woods and Forests was amalgamated with the Office of Works, in an attempt to avoid overlapping responsibilities and to improve efficiency. Charles had refused Canning's offer in 1826 to make him Treasurer of the Navy at a salary of £3,000 a year, half as much again as the Woods and Forests, but he and Harriet had then thought his present office so congenial that he declined it, not only because it was offered by Canning but also, as Harriet wrote, because 'we could neither of us bear to go & live at the end of the Strand'. In the next two years however the incessant attacks on the Woods and Forests made Charles thankful to retire from what had rather unexpectedly become a contentious and difficult post and to find a quieter haven.

10 The Duke in Power

Canning's appointment and the resignations of the Tory members of the Cabinet deprived Charles of his position in the inner circle of government but it did not put an end to his activity as a political go-between. He was still devoted to promoting Wellington's interests. After the death of the Duke of York in January 1827 he had written to urge Wellington's claims to be Commander-in-Chief, though his interference was unnecessary, for the King himself professed that it had always been his intention to appoint him. In April Charles again offered his services to intercede with the press to counter damaging reports about a supposed rift between the duke and Peel, suggesting that his old ally Street might be used. Though Harriet was 'in a fury about the . . . shameless abuse of the Duke', Wellington was contemptuous of the press: 'I hate the whole tribe of news-writers', he told Peel, 'and I prefer to suffer from their falsehoods to dirtying my fingers with communications with them.' Harriet was of a different opinion: in 1820 she advised Lord Burghersh, who complained of a libel on his wife in *The Age*, a gossip magazine, that he should consult a lawyer, and 'if the lawyer said he could not prosecute, to go and horsewhip the Editor'.

Harriet was now convinced that the King no longer had confidence in Wellington and was wholly under Canning's influence. Wellington was sure that Canning wanted him out of the way, and when Knighton suggested that he might be offered the post of Lord Lieutenant of Ireland, taking Charles as his Chief Secretary, he merely laughed and the matter was dropped. 'I have no longing for office', Charles told his son, 'and were I a little less poor I never would go into office again.'

The separation from Canning was completed when the duke resigned his post as Commander-in-Chief. Charles still hoped that the duke would be able to retain a connection with the King, and wrote to Knighton in July to suggest that a meeting might be arranged on the pretext of the duke's enquiring after the King's health. He declared that although the duke could never take office under Canning, he still felt 'the same unbounded attachment' for his sovereign, and he would like 'to feel that if the hour of danger & of trouble shd arise, there will be close to the King's side a man who has passed his life in affronting danger for the throne's sake.' There was no response to the suggestion.

Harriet was depressed by the course of events and, she wrote in June, 'I do not much like writing in my book now'. When they left for the country at the beginning of August she even considered giving up her journal, but she confessed that she was reluctant to do so in case any interesting news came her way. Unexpectedly, however, the situation changed dramatically, for three days later Canning was dead. 'Poor Mr Canning!' Harriet exclaimed in a letter to Lady Shelley.

> I am really very sorry for him . . . I cannot feel rancour against the dead; and, fatally mischievous as he has been to us, I cannot help pitying him. He has suffered so horribly, mind as well as body! . . . He was the vainest man that ever lived, with the quickest and most irritable feelings, and I know he felt his position most acutely. I have quite longed to write to Planta [his private secretary] to enquire after him; but I have not, for I should very likely have been accused of hypocrisy.

She admitted that 'he had great & brilliant talents, & one can now only feel the deepest sorrow that he shd have so misused them'.

Canning's short time as Prime Minister had not been a happy one, and his attempt to put together a 'centre' coalition of moderate Whigs and liberal Tories always seemed unlikely to succeed in the face of hostility from both Peel and Lord Grey. Nevertheless, the King determined to try to avoid capitulation to either of the old parties and appointed as Premier Frederick Robinson, Lord Goderich, nicknamed 'Goody Goderich', a weak character who had served as Chancellor of the Exchequer in the post-1822 Liverpool Cabinet. Croker called the new Prime Minister 'a vacillating, indecisive character – who did not, to quote his own phrase, know where to begin – or on which side of the sheet when he wrote a letter.' Charles thought him 'the very poorest creature that ever rose to eminence', and declared that he was even more hostile to him than he had been to Canning, who was at any rate a man of 'great powers & talents'. He advocated that the Tories should remain aloof and hold together in a body, and he was disappointed when Wellington accepted re-appointment as Commander-in-Chief, fearing that it would lead to his separation from the party. 'I fear', he wrote to Peel, 'that it will have been from us, when he came the other day to Woodford, that the Duke met with the least cordial congratulations which he has yet received.'

This was putting it mildly. Harriet remonstrated violently with the duke and they had a blazing quarrel, the duke declaring that as a soldier, rather than a politician, he could not refuse, and Harriet replying that 'it was ridiculous nonsense for him to stand up and tell me he was *no politician*' and that he ought at least to make it clear that he had no intention of giving the government his political support. 'We had a desperate *scene*', she wrote, 'for he was excessively angry, *swore* (which he never does) & said he wd do as he liked.' The quarrel was soon patched up: the duke wrote her a long letter in pencil as he drove away from Woodford and she wrote one to him in turn saying that he must excuse her strong feelings 'that we had been united politically for many years' and that she could not 'see that link severed without the severest pain' at his giving up the leading part in opposing the government. They met at the Duke of Rutland's house in Derbyshire and had a long talk while out walking and sorted it all out, though Harriet was unrelenting in her view that he should have declared his position to the Prime Minister.

Otherwise Harriet professed indifference to the ministry. 'I don't care about it', she told Lady Shelley: 'I think my political vehemence is sobering, as I advance towards more sober years.' This unlikely prophecy was not to be put to the test. Goderich was so feeble a minister that, so the story goes, he wept copiously in an audience with the King and had to borrow the royal handkerchief. 'It is a new way of governing England', Harriet remarked, and the duke pointed out that they had had all kinds of ministers except 'a *blubbering* Minister' and 'now we have got one of that sort'. Early in 1828 the ministry collapsed, and the King sent for Wellington. 'At last this most disreputable Govt has come to an end', Harriet wrote. Her dearest wish had come true, and she confidently expected that Charles would now receive the reward which was his due for his long service to the duke's interests and enter the Cabinet at last.

She was to be disappointed. Though Wellington, as he told Lord Westmorland, had consulted Charles from the moment he received his commission about every detail of the arrangements, Charles himself was not to be in the Cabinet. The King told Wellington that he wished Charles to return to the Woods and Forests and the duke offered it to him but without a seat in the Cabinet. Charles objected that 'after his long services, having been consulted & confided in', he had a fair claim to a Cabinet post, particularly since the duke had been compelled to take in the leading Canningites and the holder of the Woods and Forests had sat in both Canning's and Goderich's Cabinets. Wellington however replied that he could not have anyone in the Cabinet who was not a good speaker in Parliament, and that the office 'was not properly a Cabinet one'. When Charles persisted and threatened to resign from office altogether, the duke became annoyed '& complained of his being abandoned in his difficulties by his only confidential friend'. Charles relented but he thought it 'ill treatment after his long services & when such *rifraf* are in the Cabinet' and declared he would stay only until the end of the session unless he was put into it. Harriet was very upset. She believed that Charles was justified, but as she confided to her journal in 1823, 'it was a matter of great regret that he shd not have been more forward as a speaker in parliament, as . . . nothing is so essential to a public man in this country as the facility of speaking in parliament.' Charles admitted that his exclusion was his own fault, for not having been more active in the House, and declared that 'indeed it is very painful to me . . . never to be *mixed up* in everything, as I used to be'. However, Harriet hated the thought of an estrangement from the duke, 'the dearest & most intimate friend we have', and she spoke to him about it. He was 'as kind in his language as possible', but there was nothing to be done. No doubt Wellington, always a good judge of men as well as a devoted servant of his country, who would never allow friendship to outweigh the public interest, knew that Charles was not really of the calibre for a Cabinet post and he put the efficiency of his government above personal considerations.

Despite this disappointment, Harriet was ecstatic at the duke's becoming Prime Minister. He 'will be *really* the head of the Govt & will overlook and superintend every department', she wrote, and he will 'make every body work for their salaries'. She looked forward to 'confidence on the part of the public & renewed energy & vigour in all our commercial affairs & renewed prosperity amongst the great mass of the nation'. Wellington would be 'as much loved at home as he is now respected & feared abroad'. The reality did not quite match her expectations. The ministers were at sixes and sevens on the Catholic question which was becoming the leading issue of the day, not least in Ireland, where the Catholics under O'Connell's leadership were more restive than ever. They were also in disarray on economic policy, particularly the pressing question of modification of the corn laws, and on foreign affairs the growing tensions between Russia and Turkey and the question of the Greek revolt presented urgent problems which affected vital British interests in the Near East, as they had done in Charles's days in Constantinople. Harriet criticized Peel's ineptitude as leader of the House of Commons. She blamed him for making Wellington insist on debating talent for Cabinet offices to cover up his own deficiencies, when in fact his Canningite colleagues hardly ever spoke. She suspected that Peel was a closet liberal: 'He is for giving up every thing', whereas the duke 'is anything but a liberal or coward' and the consequence was 'very unpleasant discussions in the Cabinet' and a bad effect on public opinion. Charles could do little to help, for he too blamed Peel for his exclusion from the Cabinet and 'has never gone near him since'. The duke was still 'the only person capable of being Minister in these difficult times' but his colleagues 'are troublesome & thwart him beyond his patience'. She wished he would be *'despotic master'* in the Cabinet, for all would then be well.

The immediate crisis arose over proposals to disfranchise two corrupt boroughs, East Retford and Penryn, and to transfer their representation to new industrial or commercial districts. The Whig reformers hoped to use this as a means of gradually achieving general parliamentary reform, while the Tories resisted it as a precedent. Peel became very testy, wishing to oppose the Bill and blaming his Canningite colleagues on the front bench for deserting him. Charles and Lord Bathurst went to see him to try to calm him down but though Harriet recorded that he talked himself into a better humour, the problem remained. The government was an unhappy coalition of unreconciled differences of principle. Wellington, as he told Harriet, was 'single-handed' in the Cabinet and 'determined to . . . decide upon every question according to its merits & without any view to party', but the four Canningite ministers were always obstructive. The Cabinet staggered on in a state of crisis until the end of May, when Huskisson and Palmerston voted against their colleagues on the East Retford Bill in the House of Commons. Huskisson wrote to the duke to offer his resignation, he thought merely as a matter of form, and to his surprise the duke accepted it. The remaining Canningites followed suit, and the government was reconstituted on Tory lines. 'We are much better without them', Harriet declared, and Charles was put into a better mood by being given the office of Chancellor of the Duchy of Lancaster, though still not in the Cabinet. However, as Harriet wrote, it put him 'quite into a good humour, which he was not before', to be rid of the Woods and Forests at last. The only snag was that Peel remained Leader in the Commons: Harriet wrote that he was arrogant and bad-tempered, 'is detested by all the young men', and the House accordingly 'in a more wild, disorderly state than I ever remembered it'. She put it down to his 'low birth and vulgar manners'.

Though Harriet now thought that 'Everything is again going on quietly', the government was sitting on a powder keg in Ireland. In the summer of 1828 O'Connell was elected to Parliament at a by-election for County Clare. As a Roman Catholic he was barred from sitting in the Commons but to exclude him would spark off a rebellion in Ireland, and to call a general election would simply throw almost the whole of Ireland outside Ulster into the hands of Catholics. Wellington approached the question in his usual pragmatic way. He discussed his ideas with Harriet on a stroll in Birdcage Walk: his plan was to admit Catholics to Parliament and to all offices, on a temporary basis to start with, on condition of their taking an oath of loyalty and the Catholic priesthood being licensed and paid salaries by the government, to control their behaviour. Harriet was 'quite delighted' with the scheme and was sure it would defuse the situation. The duke, she declared, had 'inspired the whole country with such confidence in his talents, his honesty & his good sense', and his being Minister would solve all the difficulties.

Her only regret was that he seemed so tired and worn out by the pressure of business. He was so busy, she wrote, that 'except for a moment when he goes up from the H. of Lords, I now scarcely ever see him' and when he did visit 'he brings a bag full of boxes down here in the evg to read, but then he can't talk'. His 'amusements', she told Lady Shelley, consisted of 'going to the Treasury at noon, doing business till five, going to the House of Lords; dining – generally at dull places he don't care about – then reading and writing papers till he goes to bed. What a life!' Even after the end of the session he was kept in London by business and the Arbuthnots had to postpone their visit to Stratfield Saye until the autumn. He walked into Woodford unannounced in the middle of August and told them all the political news, and when he returned to London he wrote every day. At last they were able to visit Stratfield Saye in early September. The party included Peel and the Lord Chancellor, and the Catholic question was much discussed, so that Harriet could not have the duke to herself so much as usual, but he came on to Woodford on the 10th for her birthday and gave her his usual present – a diamond button this year. He stayed a week, 'remarkably well . . . and in excellent spirits' and returned to London to deal with the Russo–Turkish war. 'It is quite sad how he is kept in London', she wrote.

The Catholic question and the Russo–Turkish war were the two major issues with which Wellington had to deal. The former was politically dominant because the Tory party, on whom Wellington was dependent, though he was not their leader, was divided on the issue, while the two main parties outside the government, the Whigs and the Canningites, were in favour of liberalization. Wellington refused to see it as a matter of principle but regarded it in a purely pragmatic light. While personally disposed to continue the present exclusion of Catholics from public life he was by no means a bigoted Protestant and he was swayed rather by his conviction that the safety of the country was at stake. An Irish rebellion would be ruinous, and might lead to bloodshed on an even greater scale than in 1798. Despite (or perhaps because of) his military experience, Wellington was a humane individual to whom the shedding of blood was more than distasteful.

It was also clear that public opinion in Britain was moving towards emancipation. The House of Commons had voted in favour of motions for it four times since 1821, and only the recalcitrance of the House of Lords had defeated the proposal. As Wellington well knew, the Lords' attitude reflected not so much a stand on Protestant principles as deference towards the King who was well known to be hostile towards it. Despite his support for it when he was Prince of Wales, he had now adopted his father's hostility to emancipation, though largely for political reasons: it was bound up with his quarrel with Lord Grey and the Whigs after he became Regent in 1810. Wellington knew that the King was a coward when it came to standing up to pressure and that although he might storm and threaten he could be bullied into submission.

Wellington was not afraid therefore of George IV's attitude, and he knew that politically the King had no other resource, for the opposition parties were pro-Catholic. The real problem lay with Wellington's own followers and government. Peel, now Leader of the Commons as well as Home Secretary, and therefore responsible in the Cabinet for Ireland, had long ago pledged himself to the Irish Protestant cause – he had even been nicknamed 'Orange Peel'. He was in fact equally pragmatic in his attitude to the interests of the country but he was worried about his reputation for honour and consistency. He also happened to be MP for Oxford University, the stronghold of anti-Catholic prejudice. Among the outer ministry, though not so much in the Cabinet, there were others who were even more 'Protestant' than Peel, including some of the most prominent and high-ranking members of the aristocracy. These and their parliamentary followers, nicknamed the 'Ultras', were headed by the King's hated brother the Duke of Cumberland.

Wellington decided during the summer of 1828 that emancipation must be granted. Harriet was perturbed lest it should be granted too extensively, for she had a genuine feeling for the Anglican Protestant faith and establishment, but she could not oppose a measure promoted by her beloved duke. Charles was probably relieved – he had voted once before, in 1813, for emancipation, in the days when he was still friendly with Canning and before his marriage to Harriet, but since then he had allowed her to influence his view and he had not voted for the question again. Though he had come round to an anti-Catholic point of view it was not a bigoted one, and he was prepared to go along with the duke's strategy.

In the autumn of 1828, in the interval between the sessions of Parliament, Wellington worked out his proposals. He consulted Charles and Harriet in several conversations and Harriet copied out the memorandum which he prepared for the King. (It tested her devotion by taking six hours to copy.) Harriet approved of the safeguards for the Church which the duke suggested – that the Catholic priesthood should be allowed to operate only under a royal licence and thus under political supervision, that the lower classes of voters in Ireland, the 40-shilling freeholders, who were mostly Catholic peasants, should lose their franchise and that only more substantial landholders should vote, and that certain high offices in the state – the Lord Chancellor, the First Lord of the Treasury, the Chancellor of the Duchy of Lancaster and the Lord-Lieutenant of Ireland (all of whom controlled a degree of patronage in the Anglican Church) – should remain in Protestant hands, as should indeed the Crown itself. Finally, the duke envisaged that the Catholic Association, O'Connell's political machine in Ireland, should be forbidden.

However, it was not all plain sailing. Harriet had not entirely subdued her reservations, and when her friend the Duke of Rutland wrote to Wellington in November to express the doubts of the Tory party in general she could not help defending him. Wellington flew into a temper and declared that 'he had a right to expect that persons professing to be his friends shd have reliance in his honor & not suspect him of designing any mischief'. Harriet coolly replied that men in public life must expect to be criticized, and hinted at what she suspected, that Lady Jersey was behind his plans. This hardly improved the duke's temper:

> he said I told him always the most disagreeable things in the most invidious manner, & that he wd take care never to tell me any thing again or ask my opinion: and I, on the other hand, got at last into a passion, too, assured him I wd never tell him the truth again & that, if that was his way of behaving, he wd neither deserve a friend nor have one. In short, we had what he calls a grand breeze.

Their loud voices turned the heads of passers-by on the Mall where this incident took place. However, she wrote 'we ended as we always do', making up the quarrel and becoming good friends again.

So matters rested until the end of January 1829 when, with the session of Parliament approaching, the Cabinet held daily meetings to settle the details of the proposed Emancipation Bill. To Harriet's alarm the scheme that emerged differed in some respects from that of the autumn. In particular, the proposals for the state to license and pay the Catholic clergy were dropped – 'the two parts of the . . . plan which, I confess, appeared to me the best', Harriet wrote. 'I cannot say I am satisfied' and she wrote to the duke to tell him so. When the proposals were disclosed to the House of Lords in the debate on the Address on 8 February she went to hear the debate, in which the 'Protestant' Tory peers were 'very violent' in their opposition. When the duke, 'very much annoyed & mortified . . . came to our house afterwards' he was 'quite out of spirits'. Harriet's propensity to tell him the truth whether it hurt or not again made him cross and Charles scolded her for it, but, she

Morning . . . Night: *W. Heath ('Paul Pry'), April 1829. On the left, Wellington is reproached by Lady Jersey for his devotion to 'Woods and Forests' (Harriet). On the right, he calls on Harriet that evening 'in the Duchy of Lancaster' (to which post Charles has been moved). Harriet claims to have won his affections by appealing to his vanity and his passions, for 'heart he has none'*

told him, 'here, *en trio* with him', she could not pretend things were other than they were. She did, however, try to mollify the Duke of Rutland and the Tory Lords by assuring him that Wellington acted only by virtue of necessity and that the state of the country gave him no alternative. The two dukes at any rate were brought to talk to each other, but a third – Cumberland – was still working on the King and stiffening his resistance. Harriet tried to do the same for Wellington, telling him that 'if he quitted office now, I shd never wish to see him in again'.

Wellington found the King in a stubborn mood but he stood firm, to the point of reducing his sovereign to tears, only to have Cumberland swing him round again. 'We have had terrible work with the King', wrote Harriet, who was fighting the duke's battles in spirit. Wellington refused to give in and the King had to back down, though he held out for six hours, fortified with brandy, before he agreed to allow the Bill to be introduced into the Commons. The duke remarked that it was 'a battle like Waterloo' and he was determined to win it. Cumberland on his part almost brought the analogy to life by threatening to raise 20,000 men to march to Windsor with a petition to the King. They wouldn't find it an easy matter to get 20,000 men to do that, mused Harriet, unless they opened the alehouses for them when they got there.

Wellington had to fight his own private battle in March when Lord Winchelsea, a bitter opponent of emancipation, published 'a most offensive letter' accusing the duke of wishing to undermine religion and the Church Establishment. He refused the duke's demand for an apology and Wellington challenged him to a duel. The duke walked in to Harriet at breakfast and announced that they had just fought, fortunately without harm to either. 'I should have died of fright', if she had known beforehand, Harriet wrote, but she approved of the duke's action because it would teach people not to insult him with impunity. Charles Greville applauded her attitude: unlike Lady Jersey and other ladies who were 'very ridiculous, affecting nervousness and fine feelings' after the event, he wrote, 'Mrs Arbuthnot . . . made very light of it all, which was in better sense and better taste', though she admitted to Lady Shelley that she was 'ready to cry' when she heard the news.

In the end the Catholic Bill passed the Commons by a majority of over two to one and the Lords by a majority of over a hundred, in both cases with the active help and support of the Whigs and Canningites. Harriet was so thankful that she even praised Lord Grey's speech in the Lords as 'the finest eloquence'. The duke was in high spirits, but he could not forbear from abusing the King's conduct – he told Harriet he was 'the worst man he ever fell in with in his whole life, the most selfish, the most false, the most ill-natured, the most entirely without one redeeming quality . . . it was a long while before I cd get in a word.' She assured him that whatever the King might say, he (the duke) was the man in whom the people had confidence, that he had won 'a most brilliant victory' and that he would give 'permanent peace & tranquillity to a country which has never yet known either'. She urged him to stay in office but the duke was 'so angry he did not say much except that he wd *be d—d* if he wd stay'.

The duke's temper improved and the administration went on, but the rifts caused in the Tory party by the passage of emancipation did not heal themselves easily. The 'Ultras' now withdrew their support from Wellington and Peel, regarding them as renegades to their party and traitors to their principles, and the duke was forced to seek support elsewhere. Once again he turned to Charles, who contacted Lord Duncannon, a leading member of the Whig opposition and close to Lord Grey. They had a long conversation in which Duncannon suggested that if overtures were made to Grey, a substantial number of Whigs in both Houses would give their support. The duke's concession to the Catholics had removed a major difficulty against a coalition, and Grey and Wellington respected each other. The political world buzzed with rumours that the duke would offer the Foreign Office, which Grey was known to covet.

The King, however, was determined never to admit Grey to office. He had placed a veto on his admission when the duke formed his Cabinet and his personal hostility to the Whig leader still rankled. Harriet too found it difficult to welcome the thought of Grey in the government: she thought him 'a strange mixture of great talent & gross vanity'. In June she and the duke walked in St James's Park for an hour and a half and talked over the question, and agreed that a junction with the Whigs was desirable. Wellington, however, told her that 'he was sure it wd never suit him to have Lord Grey in his Cabinet, even if the King did not object; that he is a very violent, arrogant & a very obstinate man.' She confessed that she disliked Grey and feared that he 'wd want to dictate & lead' and there would be 'perpetual wrangling'. Besides, she reminded the duke, Grey had 'all kinds of fantastic notions' about parliamentary reform and foreign policy. 'In my judgement he is much better where he is', she declared. All that happened was that Lord Rosslyn, a close friend of Grey's, was admitted to the Cabinet, in the hope that this would smooth the future path to an arrangement. Harriet claimed that the appointment was, partly at least, due to her persuasion: 'we ought to shew gratitude to the Grey party, who have supported us most handsomely', she wrote.

Despite desultory conversations during the summer, no progress was made towards a closer junction of the parties. Lord Althorp, one of the leading Whigs in the Commons, and a keen agriculturalist and 'farming friend' of Charles, came to stay at Woodford for two days in June. He had discussions with Charles which led to some general agreement on the necessity of a closer coalition, but Harriet was horrified lest Charles was allowing Althorp to talk him round: 'I was quite out of patience with Mr A. for being humbugged by such stuff', she wrote. She remained a determined Tory and an opponent of liberal ideas. She and the duke agreed that the existing members of the government were perfectly adequate to their offices and that although he would have no objection to taking in leading Whigs if vacancies arose he would not seek a full party coalition. Harriet was relieved: she thought that the duke ought not to give way to threats of opposition and that if the Whigs wanted to come in they should 'give a fair & honest support as a preliminary to any application for office'. She was satisfied that Wellington remained the best Prime Minister in prospect and that his system of 'honest administration' without party exclusiveness was the best for the country.

These speculations were to become academic in the next year, when the death of George IV in June was followed by a number of more positive moves towards outright opposition by Grey and the Whigs. Foreign affairs provided a major source of difference between them and Wellington, and old personal animosities returned after the temporary co-operation over Catholic emancipation. The continued resentment of the 'Ultra' Tories against Wellington and his failure to bring the ex-Canningites back into his government left the duke's position weaker than ever, despite Harriet's admission that she would rather die than see him bring them back. Though the new King William IV publicly declared his intention of keeping the administration in office the political and economic situation in the country worsened during the autumn of 1830. The end was in sight for the duke's Premiership and for Harriet's political influence.

11   London and the Country

Since his younger days as a companion of Canning and other fashionable men-about-town, Charles had been fond of society and had been in some demand as a dinner guest. He had been *persona grata* even in the circle of Princess Caroline, the separated wife of the Prince of Wales through his connections with the Cholmondeleys, and he was often found at fashionable dinner tables in London. Harriet too was fascinated by high society and her marriage, though undoubtedly a love match, was especially appealing as an entrée to these circles after her rather dull family existence in Lincolnshire. It was Charles's social position rather than his more doubtful political prospects that appealed to her ambitious nature. After their marriage they became a leading couple in the upper-class social life of the time both in London and in the country during the parliamentary recesses.

The social life of the early nineteenth-century upper classes moved in a precisely-regulated circle, its movements dictated by the demands of the agricultural and sporting calendar and of the parliamentary timetable. Parliament usually met for about six months of the year, assembling in January or early February and sitting until the middle of the summer. The session usually ended in July, in time for dispersal to the country for shooting and, later, fox-hunting which were the principal sports of the upper classes. The heat and smell of London in midsummer were to be avoided in favour of the delights of the countryside. The English gentry and aristocracy were a country-bred class, residing on the estates which provided them with the bulk of their incomes, and retaining close contact with their tenants and labourers in order to preserve the bonds which held society together. Britain's avoidance of popular revolution after 1789 has more than once been ascribed to this close social linkage which was based at least partly on respect and deference from below towards a governing class who shared their interests and were conscious of some responsibility to those dependent on them. Industrial society and its great, impersonal, working-class towns were as yet almost unknown: it was significant that what little Jacobinism was present in the last decade of the eighteenth century appeared in industrial centres like Sheffield, Manchester and Norwich, and that the aristocracy's ability to contain it depended upon their retention of control in the countryside.

The English country house was therefore more than a place of holiday and recreation for the upper classes. It was in a real sense the focus and centre of local society and government, ruled over by a mainly benevolent and socially-aware aristocracy of birth and wealth. England in the eighteenth century has been described as a 'federation of country houses'. Everyone who had any part to play in the government and welfare of the country was to be found there. The round of country house visits that occupied the higher classes from summer to the new year was not merely recreational, but it provided a necessary means to keep the governors of the country in touch with each other and with the leading people whom they ruled. Even the wealthy urban and city middle classes coveted invitations to great houses, or, if they made enough money, entered the market to buy their own houses and estates. Charles's purchase of Woodford with its 600 acres was small in relation to the properties of the old aristocracy, but it placed him in the rank of a country gentleman rather than a mere career politician, and despite Harriet's lack of enthusiasm for it at first, she recognized its importance to her social ambitions.

The Arbuthnots' social year always began with a visit to Harriet's Westmorland relations at nearby Apethorpe for New Year. Lord Westmorland's birthday on 1 January was celebrated with a great ball for the guests and the servants, at which Harriet usually danced – she opened the ball with the Lord Chancellor as her partner in 1829 – and Wellington, she recorded in 1822, danced there for the first time since Paris in 1815, with Lady Georgiana Fane. The house party, which usually included Wellington and several other friends, went on to hunt and shoot during the week of the festivities. In 1822, Harriet noted, 'we had a very good run for ladies & rode very hard'.

Apethorpe, where Charles and Harriet had spent their honeymoon, was a gloomy and unprepossessing house. It was an old mansion where James I had often stayed for the hunting, built, as Peel wrote in 1833, 'exactly like a small college in Oxford' round a quadrangle, with a fine oak-wainscoted gallery one hundred and twenty feet long, a 'low, but rather a handsome room' and a large but neglected library. Forty years earlier another visitor, the restless John Byng, Lord Torrington, who spent a large part of his life travelling about the country, had found it equally neglected while the 10th Earl was away as Lord-Lieutenant of Ireland: 'a deserted seat, all weeds, no attempt at cleanliness, or improvement!' King James's bed and the tapestry hangings of the chamber were 'in the same stile he left them' and a large collection of family portraits was scattered higgledy-piggledy through the house. Lord Westmorland, Byng thought, must be 'cruelly ignorant of taste, civilities, or comfort' to have so neglected such a noble house. What

Apethorpe Hall, Northamptonshire

modern additions there were comprised 'a tea room of Lady W's' which 'vilely disfigured' the house, and 'foolish dressing rooms, French chairs, and useless tastes' and 'a silly menagerie' in front of the house. The Westmorland household was not an intellectual one: Palmerston in 1827 described the earl as an 'ignoramus'. Peel evidently found little changed: 'the house's equal in discomfort cannot be produced', he complained. King James I's bedroom had still not been touched, except that the bed had been removed and replaced by a billiard table, the library was still 'deserted, with all the books in confusion', and there were hardly any fires anywhere because of his host's meanness with the coals, while the rats frolicked in the closet in his bedroom. The house was full of 'a large family party of Fanes . . . seated round two whist tables in the drawing-room'.

Despite the lack of comfort, Charles and Harriet hardly ever omitted this regular beginning to the year – only in 1832 did they miss the New Year there, when Harriet's mother was ill and they had to stay at Fulbeck. Even then they managed to get to Apethorpe a few days later for the shooting. The shooting season continued into January, Harriet and Charles usually going to the Rutlands' at Belvoir, where again there was a tenants' ball and a great dinner to celebrate the duke's birthday on the 5th. In 1830 he and Harriet led a polonaise all over the house, 'the music preceded us & the whole scene was like a fairyland.' 'You can't think what a splendid effect it had', she wrote to Lady Shelley, 'for we were all as fine as diamonds and red coats could make us.'

Lady in morning dress, 1824

Belvoir was one of her favourite houses. 'Nothing can be more magnificent & princely', Harriet wrote, though she admitted that the interior arrangement of the rooms had 'great faults', there being 'no regular suite of rooms'. The castle had been burnt down in 1816 and reconstructed under the management of the late duchess, whom Charles Greville accused of having 'some taste but no knowledge'. Harriet, however, thought the exterior very fine and imposing and the new drawing-room, which was opened in 1829, was 'the most magnificent room I ever saw', hung with blue silk damask and decorated in the style of Louis Quatorze. It contained a marble statue of the late duchess, 'a woman of extraordinary genius & talent mixed up with a great deal of vanity & folly'. The present duchess was also a lively woman: Harriet raised an eyebrow in 1823 when, at a ball at Stamford, she danced till 4.30 a.m. 'tho' past forty & nearly a Grandmother'.

After Belvoir, the Arbuthnots went on either to the Shelleys' at Maresfield or to Stratfield Saye, to round off the shooting season before returning to London for the parliamentary session. Harriet enjoyed the open air, especially if she could go for long walks with Wellington: 'that is real enjoyment', she told Lady Shelley, 'for in these kinds of houses and parties I never can have what I consider a talk with him in the midst of twenty people'. Easter was always spent at Drayton, the Northamptonshire home of the Germains, for a family party. It was almost the Arbuthnots' second home, for they had a close relationship with Harriet's cousins. They visited the house at frequent intervals during the rest of the year, and often for Christmas before going on to Apethorpe.

The London season lasted from late January or early February until late July. 'London is beginning to fill and to be gay', Harriet noted in February 1827. Her routine was to pay visits on Mondays, Wednesdays and Fridays, to go to the opera on Tuesdays and Saturdays, and devote Thursdays to 'chance people'. It was much quieter and pleasanter before Easter, when the main social season began. 'I like society in London much better at this season than later', she told Lady Shelley. 'It is less crowded, less hot, and not so late.' She preferred smaller companies to play whist or écarté in the evenings: 'we have a society of thirty people who meet every night, & nothing can be more agreeable.' Whist was particularly popular – the Duke of York played incessantly and often with Harriet among those at the table.

The theatre and the opera were Harriet's best-loved diversions during the summer season. London in the 1820s had three 'licensed' theatres, Drury Lane and Covent Garden, which had the official monopoly of presenting plays, and the King's Theatre in the Haymarket which concentrated on opera. A few smaller non-licensed houses, like the little theatre in the Haymarket and the Adelphi, were tolerated. There was also the new English Opera (in fact, confusingly, a playhouse) in the Strand, till the house burned down in 1830. Harriet mainly patronized the three licensed theatres where the performances were generally of high quality, featuring the leading actors and singers of the day. She tried the Adelphi once in 1822 but thought the entertainment vulgar and the crowds noisy and ill-behaved. The licensed theatres attracted the higher ranks of society, though the audiences were beginning to be more widely representative as the middle classes became more prosperous, and there was always a hooligan element in the galleries. Prince Pückler-Muskau, the German traveller, was amazed at 'the unheard-of coarseness and brutality of the audiences' and attributed this to the preference of 'the higher and more civilized classes' for the Italian Opera. At the lower theatres, the most affecting parts of the tragedies or the most charming arias of the singers were apt to be drowned by raucous noises from the audience, while the patrons in the

Theatre Royal, Covent Garden, 1828

boxes or the pit might be assailed by expertly-aimed orange peel and other less savoury missiles.

At the King's Theatre in the Haymarket stricter etiquette was enforced. Earlier in the century, admission to the boxes or the pit was restricted to those acceptable to aristocratic lady patronesses such as the Duchesses of Marlborough, Devonshire, and Bedford. When the theatre came under different management admittance was easier, but it remained the rule that gentlemen had to wear knee-buckles, ruffles and *chapeaux bras* (a three-cornered hat held under the arm), and if there was a drawing-room that evening ladies and gentlemen were expected in court dress: on all occasions, Captain Gronow wrote, the audience was 'stamped with aristocratic elegance'. Invitations to the private boxes of aristocratic patrons were eagerly sought after, and Harriet's social connections ensured that these were often forthcoming.

She was especially fond of Covent Garden, now managed by the Kembles. Here Macready created a sensation as Richard III in 1819, and when Harriet and Charles went to see him with Charles Kemble and Miss Foote in May 1820 in the new tragedy *Virginius*, by James Sheridan Knowles, Harriet thought it very fine. *The Times* remarked that in this part Macready 'touched the passions with a more masterly hand, and evinced deeper pathos than we recollect on any former occasion'. The only embarrassment arose when in the dramatic denouement, as he was about to stab his beloved daughter, the knife became entangled in his Roman robes – 'but the blow, when given, was terrific'. Their evening was only spoilt by their getting into a two-hour traffic jam, caused by a party at Lady Charleville's, on the way home.

In February 1821 Harriet went to Covent Garden with Lady Bathurst and Wellington to see *Twelfth Night*. It was the night when the King paid his first visit to the theatre after the Queen Caroline affair and his enthusiastic reception marked the turning of the tide after all the demonstrations in favour of his wife. Harriet described the house 'crowded almost to suffocation, & the whole standing up & waving their hats & handkerchiefs for near a quarter of an hour.' Three days later she returned with her cousin Lady Georgiana Fane, to see the new tragedy *Mirandola* in which Charles Kemble played one of the best roles in his career. The King's re-emergence into public view continued on 20 March when he went to the Haymarket to see Rossini's *La Gazza Ladra* and was again loudly applauded by a full house and 'God save the King' was sung three times. Again Harriet was present, and described the 'quite magnificent' spectacle, with 'all the ladies . . . in diamonds & many of them in feathers'.

A week later she went with Lady Charlotte Greville to see M Albert and Mme Noblet, 'the two best dancers from Paris', appearing in the ballet *Oenone et Paris*. She did not approve, however, of the 'gross indecency' of their costumes: 'They might as well have had no clothes on, & I was astonished they were not hissed off the stage.' There were other new French dancers in the ballet a week later when she went to see Rossini's new opera *Il Turco in Italia*, which she thought 'quite beautiful'. This time, perhaps surprisingly, she did not object to the dancers' costumes, nor to the plot of the opera, though *The Times* reprobated its 'immoral tendency'. Rossini's popularity in England was now at its height and Harriet was one of his greatest admirers, although she thought he was personally grasping when he charged £50 for an evening to perform with Mme Colbran at private parties – particularly when her voice was 'completely worn out'. She also deplored his demand for £3,000 for a season directing the Opera and his failure to produce the promised new work.

Rossini was not her only operatic idol. In 1825 she attended a performance of Meyerbeer's *Il Crocciato in Egitto*, which featured Signor Velluti, the last of the great castrati. Harriet thought the music 'very pretty' but she disapproved of Velluti himself, 'the most disgusting creature I ever saw, high shouldered, sunk in the chest, immensely tall with long arms and legs and looking more gaunt and unnatural than one can conceive'. His voice she likened to a bagpipe and though she admitted his taste and talent she hoped there would be 'no more such importations from Italy, for it really makes one sick'. *The Times* shared her distaste for this 'representative of the epicene

Fanny Kemble: Lawrence

gender', and described his face as 'a painted sepulchre' and his voice as at times like 'a peacock's scream, or that of a superannuated lady scolding her servants'. An attempt to encore a trio in the first act was defeated by 'certain imitations of his voice, proceeding chiefly from the gallery'.

The opera did not monopolize Harriet's entertainment or lessen her pleasure in the theatre, and in 1829 she witnessed Fanny Kemble's triumphant début as Juliet at Covent Garden. 'She promises to be a very fine tragic actress', she wrote, despite her ungainly appearance, 'frightful feet and most immense arms'. It was as Mrs Beverley in *The Gamester* that Fanny had her greatest early success, but like Charles Greville, who confessed that 'she does not touch me', Harriet was 'not the least affected', though she had cried her eyes out when she saw Miss O'Neill in the part. She considered her acting to be too artificial and theatrical.

Private music parties were another popular diversion. Harriet enjoyed one given by Wellington in February 1824 and there was another at Northumberland House in May. On 24 June Wellington gave an even grander party attended by the King, the Cabinet and officers of State, foreign ambassadors, and a few selected English guests, which Harriet declared to be 'the finest concert I ever heard'. Rossini played and the greatest opera stars of the time, Mmes Pasta and Colbran, both famed for their parts in Rossini operas, and Signor de Begnis and his wife Claudina Ronzi, who had appeared in *Il Turco in Italia*, sang 'a most beautiful selection'. The King, who also loved music, stayed till 1 a.m. Pasta was renowned as the greatest interpreter of Rossini, and her appearance at His Majesty's Theatre, Gronow recollected, 'electrified the house'. Amateur concerts were also a feature of the social scene. There was a particularly delightful one at Kenwood, Lord Mansfield's house, in 1826 – 'I never heard more beautiful music' Harriet wrote.

As the summer approached, private balls and breakfast parties filled much of the time not given to political affairs. Balls were often given for charities, such as the Hibernian ball at the opera house in May 1822, arranged by Lady Conyngham and patronized by the King, for Irish relief. There were 2,500 people there, everyone in full dress and the boxes garlanded with flowers. The following year there was a costume ball for Welsh charities at Almack's which was 'very brilliant', attended by the royal family and 'all the prettiest girls in London'. The King too gave balls at Carlton House or at St James's Palace, where the annual summer ball was always magnificent but, Harriet thought, not well organized. She complained in 1825 that the supper was '*very bad*', with 'no French wines, bad fruit, no hot meat or soups' and, to cap it all, eaten '*standing up*', which she thought 'not very Royal' and put it down to Lady Conyngham's meanness. It was particularly provoking that Lady Jersey was 'flirting with every man she could get hold of' and trying to entice Lord Palmerston away from Lady Georgiana Fane, with whom Harriet was trying to make a match. To add to her offence she was setting her cap at Wellington and furious that she was having no success. Matters deteriorated after George IV's death: Harriet complained in 1831 that the balls at St James's were now 'like bear gardens' and attended by 'all sorts of people'. Balls were also political: the 'Radical ladies' of the opposition gave a 'Spanish ball' in 1823 which was sparsely attended, to Harriet's somewhat malicious delight. Tory and Whig societies rarely mingled, but politics entered even into the social life of the town.

Breakfasts, and parties beside the river, were a popular summer diversion. Harriet thought Lord Hertford's the best, at his villa at Richmond. In 1823 the party of over 200 went up the river by steam boat, dined, danced at a ball afterwards and returned after dark with the boat 'most brilliantly illuminated'. A few days later she and Charles returned to Richmond, visiting Kew Gardens on the way, dined, walked in the evening on the terrace, and returned by boat, 'a most delicious night' with not 'a breath of air to ruffle the waters'. Greenwich, however, was Harriet's favourite place for summer water parties. They could dine at the inn and walk in the park, 'a favourite pastime of mine', before returning by boat, seeing the river 'covered with pleasure boats as well as trading vessels' and meditating on 'the wealth & luxury of this immense capital'. In 1826 the summer was so long and hot that 'nothing is pleasant but being on the water constantly'. On one occasion Wellington dined with her and then rowed her on the river till half past nine in the evening – 'I enjoyed it excessively'. Three years later the summer was cold and wet, and though there were still the usual water parties 'we had such torrents of rain they were most of them spoilt'.

The summer was also, as now, the time for Ascot races, coupled in 1828 with a visit to Windsor to inspect progress on the rebuilding of the Castle. 'The whole population of beau monde, & all that of the lower classes', were there, Lady Holland reported, so that the meeting was 'more brilliant than ever'. London, meanwhile, was 'very festive, . . . breakfasts without end . . . and balls without end.'

Dancing was a popular pastime at other exclusive venues such as Almack's, 'the seventh heaven of the fashionable world', as Gronow described it. The lady patronesses of the rooms, including Lady Castlereagh, Lady Jersey, Princess Esterhazy and Mme Lieven, determined who should or should not be members, and their 'smiles or frowns consigned men and women to happiness or despair'. Their 'cliquism' was 'a pure despotism' and, like the Italian opera, gentlemen

A group of waltzers: a print of 1817

were expected to wear knee breeches, *chapeaux bras*, and white cravats. Even Wellington was once refused admission as he was wearing trousers. It was here that Lady Jersey in 1814 introduced the quadrille, and later the waltz was brought in to become all the rage in private houses as well as at public assemblies. In 1833 the aged Lady Salisbury, at 84, was thrown to the floor during a waltz at a Tuesday soirée: she recovered.

Summer excursions from London refreshed the spirits when the town was hot and social activity too tiring: in July 1823 the Arbuthnots went to Cheltenham, for Charles, who had been unwell, to take the waters, and in August Harriet went with the duke to Strawberry Hill where she thought Horace Walpole's medieval decorations showed 'a good deal of bad taste'. In June 1829 they visited the Salisburys at Hatfield, attending a grand dinner followed by an amateur theatrical entertainment by some distinguished guests, who Harriet thought 'played better than *real* actors', and a grand supper in the great hall. They travelled back to London at 3a.m. From 1829, after Wellington was appointed Lord Warden of the Cinque Ports, they paid an annual visit to his official residence at Walmer Castle. On the first occasion they returned from Margate to London by steam boat when 'it blew a hurricane, we were all dreadfully sick'.

The ending of the parliamentary sessions in July began the exodus from London, which was hot, smelly and unhealthy, back to the country. Charles's official duties rarely kept him in London for long after Parliament broke up and Woodford became their base for the summer and autumn, punctuated by family visits to Drayton, Fulbeck or Apethorpe. After 1823, when Charles took up the office of Woods and Forests, part of August was spent in tours of inspection of the Crown estates which provided a welcome diversion during the long recess. In 1823 they went to Gloucestershire to the Forest of Dean, visited Tintern, Chepstow and Cheltenham with Wellington, and finished the tour with a brief visit to Lord Bathurst's at Cirencester. The following year the New Forest was the destination and the Arbuthnots found their way to Mudeford and Bournemouth, where Mr Tregunwell, the founder of the new seaside resort, was rapidly developing it as a fashionable place for sea-bathing. Harriet was so charmed that they decided to take one of the cottages which were hired out for bathers the next summer.

They then went on to the Isle of Wight to stay with John Nash, the King's architect, at his East Cowes Castle. Harriet thought it a most beautiful spot and wished she could live in the south of England; she was particularly fascinated by the luxuriance of the trees, shrubs and flowers and compared them enviously with the vegetation of Northamptonshire. Nash she thought 'a very clever, odd, amusing man, with a face like a monkey's, but civil and good humoured to the greatest degree'. His wife, unfortunately, was 'a vulgar bore' and Harriet was not impressed by the local society. In contrast to the aristocratic circle at Lord Francis Gower's, where Lady Charlotte and Charles Greville provided amusing and intelligent conversation, she found herself 'reduced to silence very often' at the Nashes'. She indignantly denied Charles's accusation that she gave herself airs.

After the Isle of Wight they travelled to Portsmouth where Wellington met them and they were shown the dockyard, and witnessed the spectacle of forging the ships' anchors. This impressed Harriet greatly as the twenty or thirty men around each anchor beat the red-hot metal and made the sparks fly so much that Charles was struck by one and a patch of his skin was burnt off. Even more fascinating was the *Victory* and the spot where Nelson fell and the 'wretched hole' in the cockpit where he died. It was gratifying too to be with the duke, who was saluted by the guns on going on board and leaving the ship and cheered by the garrison and the townspeople. From there it was a short journey to Winchester to see the cathedral, which Harriet thought 'very handsome', and conveniently on to Stratfield Saye for five days.

The visit to the New Forest was repeated the following year. In 1826 the summer tour was to the north, Charles taking one of his farming tours and Harriet joining him at Newcastle. They crossed the Pennines to Lowther Castle for a week's visit, during which they travelled to

Durham. Harriet found the country very beautiful and greatly admired the cathedral which she thought superior in style to the 'Gothic', though she called it Saxon rather than Norman – the 'bit of Gothic' added at the east end was 'no improvement in my opinion'. She found the chanting of the choir in the service 'sublime' and declared such music far superior to 'all the singing of all the Vellutis in the world'. It stirred her religious feelings very deeply and led her, she declared, to contemplation of 'nature's God'. The beauties of nature itself moved her also as they travelled via Barnard and Raby Castles over the 'immense moors, which for many miles were on fire' back to Lowther, recently rebuilt in the Gothic style and more beautiful and imposing than any castle she had seen. Two days later they went to Ullswater where again the scenery was 'enchanting' and she longed to stay longer to climb all the hills and sail on the 'deep blue water'. Her love of the natural beauty of the English landscape was never more deeply stirred.

After the Lake District, they made their way back to Woodford via Liverpool, Chester, Shrewsbury, and the Forest of Dean and Cirencester again. At every stage there were delights, from the mountain roads and waterfalls from Keswick to Grasmere and Windermere, to the no less magnificent man-made exchange and docks of Liverpool and the curious old town of Chester with its 'rows' or covered walks. Eaton Hall, the recently rebuilt residence of the Grosvenors, seemed, however, 'the most gaudy concern I ever saw', more like the ostentatious display of the wealth of a 'parvenu' manufacturer than the truly grand residence of the old aristocracy. Taste was restored by a visit to the ruins of Ludlow Castle and some rides through the Forest of Dean and the Wye Valley, 'the most romantic & beautiful scenery I ever saw'. The return to Woodford was not an anticlimax, for the new additions to the house were now almost complete and the new dining-room was to be furnished and the house prepared for the reception of the duke and a large party to celebrate her birthday on 10 September.

Harriet's birthday was always celebrated at Woodford and the duke always came, bringing a present. In 1822 it was an emerald and pearl bracelet made from stones that had been given to him by a Mahratta chief to mark the first battle in India at which the duke was Commander-in-Chief and which by happy coincidence was fought on 10 September 1800. In 1827 he gave her a clock for her new dining-room and in 1828 a diamond button. His gifts were carefully chosen: in 1830 he had sent for various items from London but did not like any of them when they came, and 'begged I wd wait till he went to London to get something for me himself'.

There was usually a house party for Harriet's birthday, and the duke often stayed on for a week or two, hindering her writing in her journal, for, she wrote, he always occupied the only sitting-room in the house and as she kept her journal a secret even from him she could not write in his presence. If she left the room even for five minutes he wanted to know what she had been doing. These September days, however, were among the pleasantest in the year, for she had the duke to herself much of the time, whether riding out into the country or sitting comfortably at home discussing political affairs or listening to his fascinating stories of old battles.

In 1827 Charles was no longer at the Woods and Forests and so the summer excursion was a private one to Derbyshire, where they stayed at the Duke of Rutland's shooting lodge at Longshawe, 'a *very tiring* house, on the top of the moors, . . . not half finished', she told Lady Shelley, but when it was it would be 'the perfection of a shooting box'. It was 'as cold as Xmas – even the butter was frozen', but the duke assured her that it was a 'wholesome' climate – 'certainly if high winds are wholesome, this must be the most healthy place in England'. She rode out on the moors and went to see the men shooting, but she was captivated by the countryside, which was 'romantic to the greatest degree' and she told Lady Shelley that Derbyshire was the prettiest county of all she had seen. Visits to Haddon Hall and Chatsworth were delightful, though she disapproved strongly of the 'Bachelor Duke' of Devonshire's alterations and additions to the latter, for she thought he already had more rooms than he knew what to do with. The visit was not wholly a success, for Charles had bad shooting, the grouse being so wild he could not get near them, and Harriet had her quarrel with Wellington over his acceptance of the Horse Guards from Canning. In 1829 they visited Longshawe again, for the shooting in November, and this time there was considerable slaughter among the partridges. Rutland feared that she might be bored, 'for we had no party for her', but 'you know how good-humoured, and charming she is on all occasions' and it went off well. In September 1830 they travelled north again, to Childwall, the Lancashire seat of the Gascoynes, Lady Salisbury's family, in order to take an excursion to the year's most exciting event, the opening of the Liverpool–Manchester railway.

The party began well: it seemed, wrote Harriet, 'the most delightful [excursion] possible. The party at Lord Salisbury's was the gayest and most agreeable I ever was in; the Duke was received with an enthusiasm such as I, who have seen him in so many crowds, never witnessed.' On this, her first ever visit to the industrial north, she was fascinated by 'manufactories for every sort of glass and china', while the railway was 'worth going any distance to see. I never saw anything so fine'. The viaduct over Chat Moss was 'the most beautiful thing I ever saw' and the duke was in fine form – she had never seen him better. Charles too was greatly impressed and told his elder son that on the opening day the whole thirty-two miles of the track was lined by dense masses of people. He was characteristically nervous about travelling on the railway and had decided in the morning never to do so again, but Harriet was 'most eager for it, & I did not like to return in the carriage without her'. No doubt he held firmly on to his seat as the train covered fourteen miles in forty minutes and 'we went part of the way at the rate of thirty miles an hour'.

Charles's forebodings were to be all too sadly realized, though not in the way he had himself feared. They were with the duke in his 'magnificent car of carved & gilt wood with scarlet cloth awning' when Huskisson, who was present as MP for Liverpool, crossed the adjacent line to speak to Wellington for the first time since their quarrel and was struck by the 'Rocket' as it passed. His leg was crushed and he was left bleeding and in agony at the side of the line. Nothing, Harriet wrote to Lady Shelley, 'could give a notion of the horror of the scene'. Despite immediate assistance he died that evening. The party was persuaded to go on to Manchester to complete the day's programme, as the local magistrates were afraid of riots if the crowds were disappointed, but they did not attend the evening's festivities. If it had not been for 'this

Opening of the Manchester & Liverpool Railway, 1830, from a contemporary engraving. Wellington's ornate carriage is on the left

unfortunate accident which destroyed all our pleasure', wrote Harriet, 'it would have been the most delightful week I ever passed'. Wellington was deeply affected by Huskisson's death, particularly as he felt in some degree responsible for the incident. His friend and first biographer, G.R. Gleig, wrote that he was 'a changed man' and never afterwards travelled by train unless it was unavoidable.

After this tragedy the Arbuthnots resumed their journey homewards, pausing at the Cholmondeleys' where Harriet caustically noted 'we had more praying than anything else', and the Gowers' at Trentham, going on to Peel's at Drayton which she thought 'frightful' and where the men had some political discussions about the prospects for the next parliamentary session, which was to destroy Harriet's political hopes.

The Arbuthnots lived in the midst of a brilliant aristocratic society and Harriet in particular relished the position which they filled both in town and in the country. She loved visits and conversations, balls and dinners, card parties, boxes at the opera and the theatre, and all the diversions of high society. Yet she always kept her love of the countryside and the natural beauty of the English landscape, and always remembered the happy childhood she had spent at Fulbeck. 'I am very stupid tonight', she wrote to Lady Shelley when visiting her old home in 1828,

> but I have tired myself, walking over all my old haunts and fancying myself *a child* again! . . . I never am so happy as when I come here, and get my old Nurse to come and sit with me, and call me Miss Harriet, which she always does. I dare say you, who only see me *tirée à quatre épingles* for the balls, don't believe I have such ridiculous feelings; but it is really *quite* true.

At Woodford too she was happy even when alone with Charles, and if her one regret about their Northamptonshire home was that it was too small for entertaining great parties, there was more than enough compensation in her gardens and the farm and the quiet evenings spent together after the bustle of the city or the noise and gaiety of parties in town. This quiet reflective side of her character was not always apparent to her society acquaintances, but it was an important part of her life, and it was one of the reasons for the deep affection she inspired in Wellington. They had much in common in this respect and it largely explains the close bond which held them together. Harriet also disliked the loose morals of town life. She was quick to censure indecency of conduct, dress, or conversation in others; in 1823 she condemned the Duchess of Orléans' *Memoires*, which contained language 'which one wd think cd only be familiar with the most dissolute & abandoned women'. In 1826 she was scandalized by a report in *The Times* that she herself had attended a fancy-dress ball clothed as a man and demanded that the Attorney-General should be urged to prosecute the editor. She had in fact gone as Mary, Queen of Scots. She was indignant that Charles took the affair so calmly and she declared that 'there is nothing so offensive as a charge of indecency'. She was only partly mollified when other newspapers contradicted the report on the following day.

Yet Harriet was no prudish evangelical. Her religious faith was genuine, but her attachment was to the traditional Church of England and its observances. Lord Ashley, the evangelical reformer, appealed to her in 1828 to use her influence to prevent Wellington, as Prime Minister, being elected to 'that hell of all hells, Crockfords' the notorious gambling club, 'where the fiercest vice is made splendid and fashionable', but there is no record of her intervening, and Wellington did occasionally attend. Indeed she had something of the gambling instinct herself, and enjoyed an occasional visit to Ascot or Newmarket and was not averse to playing cards for money or speculating on the stock market. She relished the story of Lady Caroline Montagu's marriage to a Mr Calcraft, who was 'very poor and quite a ranting methodist', and who was once forbidden by his doctors to read the Bible for more than two hours a day 'as it seriously affected his brain'. She thought he might follow the example of Lord Barham when he married: 'When he got into bed he told his bride he wd read her a chapter in the Bible to tranquillize her mind! Upon which she blew out the candle . . . ' The *beau monde* of the 1820s, in which Harriet occupied a prominent part, was not composed solely of rakes, gamblers and sexual adventurers, but was already beginning to acquire those characteristic features of modesty, propriety and even puritanical disapproval of licence which characterized the mid-century and which reflected Harriet's own character. She did not live to see the Victorian age, but she witnessed its beginnings in the twenty years of her life in society after 1814.

12   Reform or Revolution?

The passing of Catholic emancipation in April 1829 marked the real beginning of the era of reforms which was to dismay both Charles and Harriet and to end the Premiership of the duke, their political lodestar. Emancipation had been the central political programme of the Whig opposition since the beginning of the century, but the issue divided the Tories into two groups. Those who followed Wellington and Peel were willing to put necessity before principle, and to concede what could no longer be sensibly resisted in order to ensure the continuance of Tory government. A substantial section of the Tory party nevertheless refused to sacrifice what they saw as the essential core of the British constitution, the close alliance of the Church of England and the State. To break the monopoly, however theoretical, of the Anglican Church as the established religion of the country was to open the floodgates to radical change and to threaten the nature of the monarchy itself.

However, Catholic emancipation was not so much a cause as a symptom of change. Reform was in the air: political, economic and social, as well as religious life was poised for change in a world no longer dominated by the old landed ruling class. In the new industrial districts particularly, the middle classes were demanding a share of political influence to match their rising economic power. The Tories were increasingly seen as standing for an old, outdated order of society. The Whigs, even under the leadership of aristocrats like Lord Grey and the Dukes of Devonshire, had attracted the support of self-made men of a radical disposition like Henry Brougham, and the younger generation of more progressive and educated scions of nobility like Lord Althorp and Lord John Russell were prepared to respond to the new demands, provided they did not go too far towards the democratic radicalism of Hunt and Cobbett. These younger men in the Whig party persuaded Grey to abandon his attitude of 'benevolent neutrality' towards Wellington, and after over a decade of relative inactivity the Whigs again prepared to take up the cause of reform.

In April 1830 the situation began to change. George IV's health began to give way, bringing the prospect of a new reign and the lapse of the royal veto on Grey, and at the same time the economy began to deteriorate and agricultural distress began to create unrest and disturbances in the counties. Charles at first dismissed these reports as merely put about by the Ultras to harass the government, but as time went on the news from the countryside began to look ominous. More immediate, however, was the fear for the King's health, and during June more and more alarming reports were heard. At the end of the month he died, and the crisis began.

Harriet's verdict on George IV was a just one. He was, she wrote, 'a strange creature', a mixture of kindness and selfishness, clever but lazy, fond of the arts but 'with the most infamous taste'. He had few friends but 'never did much harm'. The Arbuthnots had experienced his kindness and generosity when they were in need of financial help, and his friendship in the social milieu, and Charles had served him loyally in office. They were never to be so close to the new King, William IV, who was generally regarded as an amiable and ineffective buffoon, though he was often more conscientious than his late brother in performing his royal duties. For them, the death of George IV marked the end of an era.

It also began a new age of reform. William at first announced his entire confidence in and support for Wellington, but he did not share George IV's rooted objection to taking Grey as his minister, and though he quickly became alarmed at the extent of Grey's reform plans he found himself unable to sustain any alternative to the Whig ministers who took office in November 1830. That event marked the fulfilment of all the fears which Charles and Harriet had for the future. To them, reform on the scale now threatened was tantamount to social as well as political revolution.

Grey and the Whigs, sensing their opportunity, hardly waited for George IV to be laid in his grave before committing themselves to outright opposition to Wellington's government, and though the general election – which had to be held in the summer – made little difference to party strengths in the Commons, the Whigs were able to ride on the incoming tide of public opinion. Fanned by the inspiration of another revolution in France against the absolutist government of Charles X and Polignac – with whose political attitudes Wellington was rather unfairly associated by much of the public – enthusiasm for reform blazed up anew in Britain during the autumn. Urged on by Charles and Harriet, Wellington attempted to strengthen himself by readmitting the ex-Canningites to office after Huskisson's death, but they decided that their prospects were better with Grey. When the new Parliament assembled in November, the opposition at once raised the question of parliamentary reform, and Grey made it the theme of his first speech on the address. Wellington, in replying to the debate, committed his major blunder by declaring that not only would his government not introduce reform, but there was no possible improvement that could be made to an already perfect system. Two weeks later the ministry was defeated by twenty-nine votes in the Commons on the proposed civil list for the new monarch, and the government fell.

The news of the defeat was unexpected. Harriet was dining at Apsley House in a large party on the evening of the division when Lord Worcester came in with the news. Wellington at first believed that the majority was on the government's side, and was only surprised that it was so small. When he was undeceived he concealed the fact from all his guests except Harriet, to whom he whispered the news before she and the company departed. The following morning he went to the King and resigned.

Harriet wrote that she was 'vexed to death' at the duke's defeat, after all he had done for the country. She confessed that 'excepting my husband & his children, I have no feeling of warm interest for any human being but the Duke' and she was 'mortified beyond expression' on his account. 'I shall write very seldom now, I dare say, in my book', she wrote a week later, 'for, except the Duke, none of the public men interest me.' She kept up her journal for another fourteen months, but the entries became shorter and more intermittent, and stopped in mid-sentence on 17 January 1832. Whatever the reason for the interruption, she never had the heart or the interest to take up her pen again, even during the exciting 'days of May' when the struggle over the Reform Bill reached its height. 'The Duke's Govt is ended', she wrote in December 1830, 'which was the only thing I really cared about in public life'. It was some consolation that Wellington was happier out of office than he had ever been since he became Prime Minister, and their social intimacy was never interrupted. But the prospects for the country seemed totally black, as the riots and disturbances which accompanied the struggle for reform even reached Woodford, and the duke's windows at Apsley House were broken so often that he left them unmended for eighteen months. She despaired of the Tories ever making an effective opposition, let alone ever becoming the government again. She declared that the duke had 'lost heart entirely', and he thought 'the revolution is begun and . . . nothing can save us.' Everything was at the mercy of the 'mob' and 'England is gone perfectly mad'.

If Harriet was despondent, Charles was overwhelmed. In April 1830 he told Lord Cowley that he was 'tired of public life' and if it were not for his obligations to the duke he would willingly 'sacrifice income & everything else for tranquillity & retirement'. In February he had written to Peel that he thought the prospects in the House of Commons were gloomy, and that 'what I want is to stay in with honour, or to go out without disgrace', but if the government fell 'it wd break my heart'. His sole desire in remaining in office, he wrote in July, was 'to see the Duke and you triumphant'. He was prepared to slog along if the government could be made effective, perhaps by a coalition with the Canningites or even the Whigs, at the price of conceding a degree of reform, but the duke's declaration against all reform ended any hopes on that score. 'If one looked solely to personal comfort the sooner the coup de grace was given the better', he wrote on 5 November, 'but it is very galling to be defeated, & with an Ultra Liberal Govt in France what a prospect for England if we are now to have the convulsion of a change here at home!'

The duke's resignation in fact ended Charles's official career, and the blow was doubled in December when he lost his seat in Parliament on the Speaker's decision that he could not hold it while drawing a public pension. 'We are now threatened with ruin', he wrote to his son. The situation was made worse by the parliamentary enquiry into public pensions instituted in December 1830 by Joseph Hume and other radical MPs, which aroused Charles's nervous fears for his remaining income. His diplomatic pension of £2,000, granted after his return from Constantinople in 1807, had been held in abeyance while he occupied government office between 1809 and 1830, when, he declared, he left public life poorer than he had entered it. Now his pension, together with the £1,200 granted to Harriet in 1823, was all they had to live on, and if either sum was lost they would be in penury. He asked Peel to look after his interests if the pensions were questioned. 'I wish to stand well with the Public because I hope that I deserve it', he wrote. Characteristically, however, he could not help fretting nervously lest anything should go wrong, and he even warned Harriet not to criticize Althorp or any of the ministers in public 'until the pensions are over – you are quoted whether you speak or do not speak' he wrote, and an indiscreet word might compromise their chances of being left alone. Harriet's pension was referred to in the Commons when the enquiry was set up, and though she declared that she did not believe there was any danger Charles was in a great fidget. He wrote of Althorp as 'that Jacobin' and the Whigs as 'the veriest blackguards that ever breathed'. He confessed that his nerves were 'shattered' and 'Often do I wish that I had never been concerned with political life', but 'once the pension question [is] over, . . . there will be nothing to care about.'

Charles's old colleagues in the Commons did their best to protect him. John Charles Herries, who had been in Wellington's Cabinet, assured Charles that they had deliberately avoided discussion of any individual pensions and that 'nothing had passed to require any vindication of character, & that the House had shewn no ill temper in

Radicalism and Incivility, or The Fair Pensioners: *John Doyle ('HB'), 24 January 1831. 'John Bull' (right) demands to know the reason for the pension granted to Harriet, who is drawn forward by a mysterious figure in a high cocked hat*

Throwing a light on the dark deeds of the pensioners, *published by W. Maclean, 1831. Lords Brougham and Grey, as constables, shine their lanterns on a group of pensioners found robbing the Treasury, while Lord Holland brandishes a blunderbuss marked 'Reform'. The dark woman standing may be Harriet*

respect of the individuals whose names had been mentioned.' They had confined themselves to the general constitutional question of interference with the King's prerogative of granting honours and rewards from the civil list, subject only to Parliament's right to set an overall limit to the sums involved. He thought there was no danger of cancelling any existing pensions, and no 'evil spirit in the House . . . beyond the cowardly desire of many of the members to curry favour with their constituents by manifestations of anti-corruption, as they are pleased to call it.'

The threat to Charles's income, and even more to his peace of mind, rumbled on for another three years, casting a further cloud over the dismal prospects which Charles divined for the country. During the discussions he received several anonymous letters. 'I do despond most dreadfully,' he told his son in March 1832; it 'cuts me to the quick' to end his days as a pensioner. 'I had made my own way in the world. What I got was got, I thought, honourably; & now to be turned round upon & to be considered the scum of the earth because I have been compensated for my services is more than I can bear. It causes me to hate showing myself anywhere. . . . I do assure you it drives me out of society, & often makes me feel that the grave is my only refuge.'

These feelings were as much the consequence of the state of the country during the passage of the Reform Bill as of Charles's personal situation. In the autumn of 1830 riots and rick-burnings in the agricultural counties expressed the desperation of the labourers in a time of economic distress and shortage of work. Threats were made against landowners, farmers, and the clergy in attempts to secure reform of the poor laws and to outlaw the use of threshing machines which reduced the demand for labour. Harriet was inclined to be dismissive at first, blaming not the state of the economy but the activity of people who 'make it their business to excite the passions of the lower orders' and the supineness of magistrates who feared to punish those responsible for agrarian crimes. She admitted that in some areas the 'peasantry . . . do really suffer under great privations' but she attributed the violence to 'incendiaries & agitators' who lauded the French Revolution and urged the lower orders to rise in rebellion. Charles received threats that the 'mob' was coming to Woodford to attack his threshing machine but Harriet refused to believe that their own labourers were discontented and attributed it to 'vagabonds . . . come from a distance' to stir up trouble. Charles nevertheless set off for Northamptonshire with his son, who as a Lieutenant Colonel had experience in commanding and organizing forces, taking two servants, four soldiers and a supply of arms and ammunition. On arrival at Woodford they were met by 'ghastly looks' and heard 'shoutings &

yellings' at a neighbouring farm. They at once set to work to melt down lead to make bullets – their ammunition had not yet arrived – loaded their muskets and walked over to the farm buildings where the mob was gathering and shouting. They decided that they had insufficient force to defend the farm as well as the house, so concentrated on the latter. Charles asked Harriet, who had stayed in London, to consult the duke as to whether it would be legal to fire on the mob if they attacked the threshing machine. He and his son also set about raising the morale of the neighbouring landowners, and Charles organized and chaired a meeting which resolved to form an association for mutual support. 'I believe it is lucky I came down', Charles wrote, 'for now the Country is [in] heart & spirit, & upon my honour it was in a frightful state, no one knowing how to act & no one daring to act. We are now I trust in God quite safe. . . . Charles was beautifully collected, & arranged our plans so that even with our few servants alone we wd have defended the house. . . . I shall have a good night's sleep.' Charles's son paid equal tribute to his father – 'everything is owing to my father who has exerted himself to the greatest degree.' As at Constantinople over twenty years before, Charles showed that however nervous and hesitant he might be in ordinary times, he was capable of decisive action in emergency.

The crisis was not quite over, however. Charles returned to London but left his son in charge of the defence of Woodford. Threats were made against Charles for his role in apprehending some of the rioters, and a man tried to fire five corn stacks one night but was frightened off. He went to the Horse Guards to try to persuade the Commander-in-Chief to keep troops of infantry and dragoons in the neighbourhood, but was told that the local commander believed the emergency to be over. It was also pointed out that there were difficulties in provisioning small numbers of soldiers who would be scattered about and he concluded that the best defence lay in the activity of the landowners in the association he had helped to set up. He told his son to let it be known that 'under no circumstances of intimidation will I while life is in me yield to the dictation of a mob' and urged him to set up a watch system against further activity. The disorders died down after the winter as they did elsewhere, when the level of distress decreased and the government took drastic action to prosecute and execute or transport many of the labourers who had been involved.

More serious than the scattered agricultural disturbances of 1830–31 was the threat of organized riots and disorders in the towns and cities during the struggle over the Reform Bill. Wellington's declaration against parliamentary reform had aroused hostility among the middle and lower classes: as well as signing the death warrant of his administration, it had made him personally unpopular, and a target for

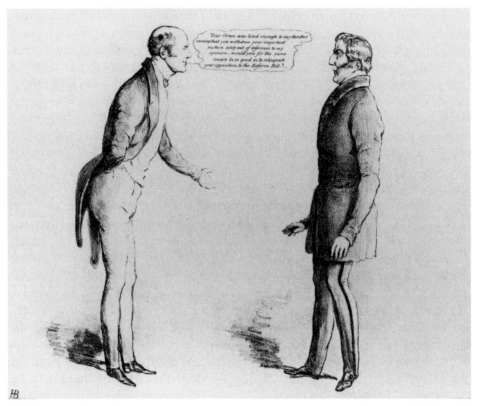

A Modest Request: *J. Doyle, 23 March 1832. Lord Grey asks Wellington to give up his opposition to the Reform Bill*

the London mob. Whether or not the Tory opposition could be reunited and strengthened and even resume control of government, the country was now so determined on reform that even the duke could not have resisted it. The introduction of the first Reform Bill in March 1831 was soon followed by a narrow defeat for the government in the Commons but when the ministers responded by dissolving Parliament they were swept back into office by a landslide vote. By the autumn, the Bill had passed through the lower House by large majorities, leaving the House of Lords as the only hope of the anti-reformers and, consequently, the target of public demonstrations designed to force the peers to give way.

Harriet and Charles did not waver in their conviction that the Reform Bill was the beginning of a revolution and that the duke must stand firm to defeat it in the Lords. 'Billy' Holmes, the opposition Chief Whip, urged them to come to town in September as they could be 'of great use to the cause in the Lords'. Harriet was optimistic that despite the fact that 'England is gone perfectly mad . . . in their desire to have this nonsensical Bill', the Lords would stand firm and throw it out. She was heartened by the debate on the second reading in October which she declared was 'excellent & well calculated to prove that an hereditary legislature is well capable in point of talent, constitutional knowledge & firmness of purpose, to compete with the Lower House. . . . I don't believe there ever was a debate that did more credit to a legislative assembly.' The government was defeated by forty-one votes, the majority including twenty-one of the twenty-four bishops. The consequence was an outbreak of rioting all over the country, including the burning of several bishops in effigy on 5 November in place of Guy Fawkes. Apsley House was a particular target, the crowd hurling stones through the windows for over fifty minutes before a single policeman appeared. The front and side windows of the house were destroyed, and one stone almost hit the duke on the head in his sitting-room. After the attack the area between his room and the garden was filled with stones. In the provinces there were even more serious disturbances, with large parts of Bristol, Derby and Nottingham being destroyed by fire. It almost seemed as if the Revolution was about to begin.

Harriet nevertheless believed that all was not lost. The Reform Bill could hardly be forced through the Lords without the creation of a large number of Liberal peers to outvote the opposition, and she did not think the ministers would venture on so great and controversial a step. If the duke managed his forces adroitly, he 'will carry any measure he pleases' and there were still 270 in the Commons who 'feel that their lives & properties are at stake', with others who might be 'open to conviction as to the absurdity of . . . the Bill' and its 'dangerous tendency of . . . spoliation'. Her only worry was that the Tories lacked leadership, while the duke and Peel were so bitter about the treatment they had received from the Ultras that there was little hope of the restoration of Tory unity. She even allowed herself for once to criticize the duke, who she thought had become bad-tempered and unable to tolerate disagreement with his views. With all his fine qualities, he seemed to hang back, 'disgusted with having been the victim of a faction' and unwilling to act decisively. In the Commons Peel, despite his display of 'consummate ability & powers of speaking' in the last session, was 'supercilious, haughty & arrogant' and defective as a leader. There was little to be hoped for from the King, who was the dupe of his ministers and afraid to obstruct them despite his hatred of them and their Bill. Her only real hope was that the ministry would collapse because of its internal disagreements, but though the Cabinet was at loggerheads over the creation of new peers there was little real prospect of the failure of the Bill.

Hopes were revived in May 1832 when the Lords carried a wrecking amendment against the Reform Bill and the King finally refused Grey's

Dame Partington and the Ocean: *J. Doyle, 24 October 1831. Wellington as Mrs Partington, who tried to turn back a flood at Sidmouth in 1824, wields a mop in vain against the tide of reform, in which the faces of Russell, Althorp, Brougham and Grey appear*

Taking an Airing in Hyde Park: *J. Doyle,*
10 June 1833. Wellington stares out of
Apsley House whose windows, frequently
broken during the Reform Bill agitation,
were still unmended in 1833

request to make new peers and accepted his resignation. 'The great joy is that they *are out*' Charles wrote to his son. Wellington was commissioned to form an administration and the country watched anxiously for the fate of reform. The radicals organized a run on the Bank of England, with the slogan 'To stop the Duke, go for gold!' but there was as yet no repetition of the riots of the previous autumn. 'The D. of Wellington wd rather burn his hand off than not try to save the King, & he is ready to make the attempt', Charles wrote, while the King was 'as stout as a lion'. Realism prevailed, however, when Peel declined to join the proposed administration, knowing that the Whig majority in the Commons could not be overcome and refusing to tarnish his reputation still further by passing a modified Reform Bill, which would be another betrayal of principle like that over Catholic emancipation. Wellington confessed his failure in the Lords on 17 May and Grey was recalled to office. Harriet attended the debate and told Charles 'the Duke was admirable' in defeat, but defeat it was. The King had to promise to create whatever number of peers was necessary to pass the Bill, and rather than see the House of Lords so humbled by such a step Wellington and his leading colleagues stayed away from the final proceedings and allowed the Bill to pass. 'Nothing can be well worse', Charles wrote to his son, 'short of actual revolution, & nothing but the Providence of God can save this ill-fated Empire.'

Charles and Harriet were convinced that the country was ruined, and the Tory party crippled for ever. 'I consider the revolution as begun', wrote Charles. 'At my age I cannot expect to see my country in prosperity again. It drives me frantic.' The 'poor weak man the King' had 'given the whole power to a fierce democracy ready to destroy him & all else with him. I have not a single ray of hope . . . .' During the 'days of May' he had thought it necessary to advise his son to 'be calm. If the Radicals rise I need not desire you to put them down. But do it with calmness as well as firmness . . . and above all should there be effusion of blood stop it as quickly as you can, for after all they are our fellow-creatures & countrymen, & are not so much to be blamed as the wicked Ministers who have deluded & excited them.' A month later he repeated that 'These wicked men have destroyed Public Prosperity & private Happiness. I am sure they have destroyed mine completely . . . & my only hope is now in Providence.' He retired to Woodford to escape 'all the Croakers who fill my room from morning till night. . . . In the country I shall not be talking all day long of our sad fate, tho' the driving it from my mind will be impossible.'

His anxieties about money kept cropping up: 'I do assure you it is most painful to me not to let you have plenty of money at all times', he wrote to Harriet who had stayed in London, 'I never spend a shilling that can be saved. I dined yesterday on Bacon & Eggs . . . ' He longed to be with Harriet but 'I shall not wish you to come while London can have any charms for you'. The house in Carlton Gardens, however, would have to be sold, for there was little point in coming to town now that the duke was no longer at the centre of affairs and, as Harriet wrote to Lady Shelley from Woodford, 'I am here now *for ever*, unless something wonderful happens; so you had better write me all the news and gossip you know.'

Even Wellington shared this despondent mood. 'You have no idea how detestable London is', Charles told his son in March 1833, hearing from the duke 'from morn till night that we are going fast the way the French went 40 yrs ago . . . ' The government's proposal to abolish flogging in the army was another sign of the times. Wellington feared that the discipline of the troops could not be preserved without it, and Charles echoed his views, telling his son that although 'perhaps to a fault & to weakness I have a horror of ever inflicting it, without the power the discipline of the army is gone.' The duke, Charles wrote to Harriet, 'certainly is Job's comforter' in these trying times.

The setting up of a Parliamentary enquiry into the Woods and Forests office further depressed him, especially when one member moved a motion of censure against him for improperly authorizing an advance of money for building the Duke of York's house when all he had done was what the Treasury ordered. 'You see . . . how glad they wd be to injure me', he told his son. The pensions enquiry too was still going on. 'Really we are all in such a state of ruin', Harriet wrote to Lady Shelley, 'with every sort of horror hanging over our heads, that I never can bring myself to write a letter. . . . In my judgment nothing can exceed the exquisite folly, knavery, and vulgarity of the Ministers and their worthy allies in the *reformed* House of Commons.'

The prospect of further trouble over the pensions in the 1834 session brought out all Charles's resentment and despondency: 'To be so abused for what the King had a right to give, & for wh. I passed a long life of hard labour, is hard & unjust', he wrote to his son. 'I have never for the last 3 years had any peace . . . could I afford to give up the pensions I wd tomorrow, for they are my misery.' Though Harriet refused to be as agitated as her husband, '& treats the attacks with sovereign contempt', Charles could not avoid fretting. On 18 February a member attacked Harriet's pension by name, asking what services she had rendered the country in return for the receipt of £9,365 of public money, and his motion was lost by only eight votes. Charles consulted Wellington about a statement he proposed to send to Lord Althorp, and the duke assured him he had nothing to fear. Althorp's response was not unfriendly: the attacks, he wrote, come from 'persons not as well inclined to you & her as I am' and he declared that Charles's services to Liverpool and his earlier diplomatic services fully justified the pensions: the only delicate point was that they had two pensions, and not one. 'You hate my politics', Althorp wrote, 'you think I have ruined the country, but I believe you do not dislike me personally.' Charles was still nervous, and hardly slept during his stay in London for the debates, but the end came, to his great relief, on 5 May when the enquiry was voted down by a large majority and Harriet's pension was never even mentioned.

So the last Parliamentary session of Harriet's life passed off without damage, and in the summer of 1834 they could celebrate without anxieties the duke's installation as Chancellor of Oxford University, which was to be the last great event of her life.

13 Life without Harriet

The death of Lord Grenville, the veteran political leader, in January 1834, vacated the Chancellorship of Oxford University, still the stronghold of High Church Toryism in an increasingly liberal world. The election of his successor was very much a political affair, and chief among the names canvassed were those of Peel and Wellington. The duke was surprised that he should be considered: not only had he had to remove his two sons from Oxford after some mischievous pranks at Christ Church, but he himself was very conscious of his lack of higher education or of intellectual accomplishments. Grenville had been a brilliant scholar and one of the leading classical authorities of the day: Wellington declared that he 'knew no more of Greek or Latin than an Eton boy in the remove' and that he was therefore 'incapable and unfit' for the headship of the foremost home of classical learning in the kingdom. His success in life had been achieved 'without academical education' and he was more an example to be avoided than imitated by undergraduates.

Nevertheless, he could not conceal his pride at being so recognized by such an eminent institution as Oxford, in theory at any rate, and the political dimension was particularly apposite. He did suggest that Peel would be a more appropriate candidate – he had a double first, had served as MP for the University until compelled to give up the seat during the furore over Catholic emancipation, and would have welcomed the endorsement of his political integrity by a return to favour at the University. But when his sponsors persisted, the duke had no hesitation in accepting nomination and Peel withdrew, so as not to deepen the divisions in the Tory party.

The withdrawal rankled, however, and the already strained relations between the two Conservative leaders after the events of 1832 deteriorated still further. Charles resumed his accustomed role of mediator, and Peel was invited to dine with the Arbuthnots and Wellington on the duke's birthday, but, Charles told Lord Aberdeen, the two men hardly exchanged a word. Wellington tried to soothe Peel's ruffled feelings by telling Charles – knowing that it would be passed on – that in the event of the Tories returning to office he would wish Peel to be Prime Minister, and would seek no office himself save perhaps the

Horse Guards. Peel was mollified, but not sufficiently to attend the duke's installation in June.

Charles and Harriet were among the guests invited to witness the celebrations at the duke's installation, which lasted four days. The almost militant Toryism of the occasion certainly appealed to them, and Harriet sought every opportunity to appear in Wellington's company, to the extent that she elicited the frowns and displeasure of both Oxford fellows and spectators from London. She put herself forward to walk about the streets with him every morning and, as Lady Salisbury disapprovingly noted, 'she tried to monopolize him as much as she could, but he did not encourage it'. She was not so much thrusting herself into the limelight as revelling in the homage paid by the crowds of all classes to her hero: to her, it marked the duke's greatest triumph and symbolized what she believed, the underlying Toryism of the people of England against the machinations of radicals and liberals in London.

Among the numerous ladies who travelled to Oxford for the ceremonies were many other well-known society figures and friends of Harriet. Princess Lieven, Ladies Salisbury, Jersey, Clanwilliam, and the Duchess of Buccleuch were only the most prominent. They

A Promising Pupil: *J. Doyle, 1834. Wellington takes lessons in Latin pronunciation from Sir Henry Halford and J.W. Croker*

The Chancellor of the University of Oxford: *J. Doyle, 1834. Wellington as chancellor in procession attended by Charles Bagot, Lord Fitzroy Somerset, Lord Hill, Sir Henry Hardinge, the Marquess of Londonderry and (second from left) Sir Henry Fane*

walked to the various events in their finery, providing Oxford with a fashion parade which was, as Croker remarked, 'the wonder of the day'. The ladies wore morning dresses 'with small bonnets of a thousand colours, and ten thousand varieties of fashions', outshining 'any court dresses I [Croker] had ever seen'. On the first day, when honorary degrees were to be awarded in the Sheldonian, the crowd was packed tightly into the theatre and cheers and loud applause greeted the appearance of the most well-known and Tory personalities. Wellington was naturally the most applauded, the clamour lasting for ten minutes. The general atmosphere, wrote Lady Salisbury, was 'of the most decided Tory kind', so that 'even *I* feel almost too liberal for the air of this place'. The undergraduates, packed into the gallery, enjoyed themselves, rather like a modern Promenade concert audience, in calling out the names of prominent persons and shouting appropriate political slogans with 'suitable hissing or applause'. The hissing was reserved for Lord Grey and the ministry, the loudest applause for 'the Bishops' and Cumberland, next to Wellington himself. When the candidates for degrees, Wellington's old military colleagues and Tory politicians, were presented the duke had to read out the Latin formula, for which he had been rehearsed by Sir Henry Halford, the physician,

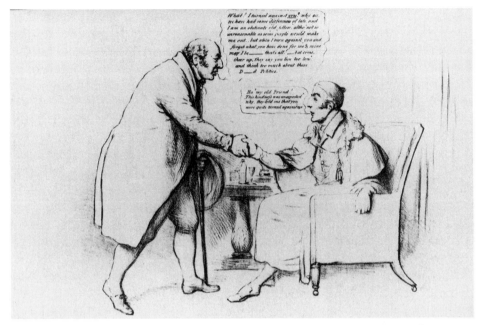

For Auld Lang Syne: *J. Doyle, 28 December 1831. Wellington, recovering from an illness at Walmer, is visited by 'John Bull', who declares his admiration for him despite his opposition to reform*

whom Wellington had consulted as 'most likely from his prescriptions, to know Latin'. Despite a few false quantities, he did it very well.

After these proceedings there was a luncheon at All Souls, attended by the ladies, and later a dinner for the men at University College with the Vice-Chancellor. The ladies enjoyed a buffet or 'pic-nic' in the coffee room at the Angel. In the evening Lady Salisbury gave a *soirée* for the duke at the hotel.

On the following day the scenes of enthusiasm for the duke were redoubled. The gallery was in even noisier form, calling out such cries as 'Whigs and pickpockets!' and 'Tories and honest men', hissing Grey, the ministry, the reformed Parliament and 'French allies', and greeting with violent applause all references to the bishops, the House of Lords, 'the memory of George 3rd' and the continued barring of Oxford to dissenters. There followed the installation ode, composed by John Keble, which Croker thought 'bad music to worse verses', and the Newdigate prize poem, recited by its composer Joseph Arnauld. At the lines which referred to Wellington as the victor of Waterloo, Lady Salisbury wrote, 'the whole theatre seemed one living mass that rose in concert . . . the noise was positively astounding and continued fully quarter of an hour. . . . they roared, they screamed, they waved hats and handkerchiefs, they actually jumped and danced with delight.' 'The ladies and the grave semicircle of doctors became as much excited as the boys in the gallery', Croker wrote. Wellington sat impassive, for the reciter was on his deaf side and he had not heard the words. In the evening the grand installation dinner was given in Christ Church hall, followed by a ball at the Star which Lady Salisbury described as 'the most frightful crush I ever beheld'.

On the fourth day there was another degree ceremony at which, Lady Salisbury wrote, the enthusiasm was not 'the least diminished'. The duke performed his part 'admirably well', though he had some difficulty in doffing his hat and occasionally resorted to a military salute. There followed a 'great breakfast' at half past three in All Souls library, at which Harriet was observed to be rather too prominent, with dancing, mainly Scottish reels, 'which must have startled all the musty old authors on their shelves', the doctors in their scarlet robes and the young noblemen in 'gaudy gowns . . . adding prodigiously to the effect'. After dark they repaired to the Angel for a final soirée and departed the following day after more sightseeing. It was, wrote Lady Salisbury, 'the most delightful week I ever spent', and seemed like 'a fairy vision of beauty and delight'. Harriet told Lady Shelley how much she had enjoyed the occasion: after 'having seen the Duke pelted, and hooted in a way that made me *hate* England and Englishmen for the past few years, it gave me new life to witness again an enthusiasm that, strange to say, was greater than I ever witnessed – even during the year after the Battle of Waterloo'. Oxford seemed a bastion of future Conservatism, particularly as Cambridge during the ceremonies had elected a liberal MP. Wellington's presence as Chancellor of Oxford was entirely appropriate, and for Harriet and Charles must have reawakened feelings of hope for the future.

Those hopes were to be cruelly snatched away only seven weeks later. During the struggle over the Reform Bill the cholera had arrived in north-east England, carried aboard a ship from the East, and in the following months it spread rapidly to almost all parts of the country, carried, though no one knew it at the time, by impure water supplies. Charles was inclined to play down the danger of the disease, writing to his son that 'my fears are so completely *moral* that I have no room for any that are merely *physical*'. His 'greater horror' was of '*The Reform. This* poisons my life.' Harriet too noted in her journal in December 1831 that the cholera had arrived in Sunderland but 'I think it a far inferior evil to the Reform Bill.' It was a tragic misjudgement.

Soon after their return from Oxford they set out to Woodford for the summer, with Harriet 'in high health and spirits' as Thomas Raikes recorded. She had longed to go abroad for July and August, to go up the Rhine and meet the Shelleys in Switzerland, but as usual Charles was

A Sketch in the Park, *1834. Wellington and Harriet by an unknown artist (? d'Orsay),*
published six days before Harriet's death

impossible to shift. 'I fear it would be less difficult to move a mountain than my husband', she wrote. While at Woodford she was suddenly taken ill with a stomach disorder which had all the signs of an attack of cholera but on the second day she was reported to be recovering. She went out walking to a nearby farm on Saturday 2 August, was again seized with violent stomach pains and collapsed. Sir Henry Halford, who had been attending her, was sent for, but when he arrived she was dead.

Her death was a terrible shock to all her friends, but especially to Wellington. He was in London for a debate in the House of Lords, and spent the evening at the Salisburys'. Lady Salisbury wrote that he arrived 'in high spirits', and pleased with the news of Harriet's apparent recovery. Just after her bedtime an express messenger arrived with the news. Lady Salisbury recorded the scene as told by her husband:

> He threw himself in the greatest agitation on the sofa . . . and the letter on the floor: and then rose and walked a few minutes almost sobbing about the room, after which he retired. In the morning Lord S. got a note from him saying he must go to Mr Arbuthnot – he left for Woodford about half past eight on Sunday morning.

It was typical of Wellington's concern for others, even in the time of his own distress, to think of going immediately to Charles, knowing that he would be devastated. To be a widower for the second time after two exceptionally happy marriages was almost too much to bear, especially since the political events of 1830–2 had already reduced him to a state of depression. He suffered what seems to have been a nervous breakdown. He could not bear even Woodford, where they had spent their times alone together, and as soon as he was able to travel the duke took him into his own house. Woodford was made over to Charles's son and apart from occasional visits and family Christmases he spent the rest of his life with Wellington, two men growing old together in a tightly-knit companionship cemented by their memories of and love for Harriet.

Four years later, on the eve of the anniversary of her death, Charles wrote to his son of his feelings about both his marriages: of his first wife, Charles's mother,

> a more perfect angel in form & mind was never seen on earth. . . . She has never been out of my thoughts, & it has invariably been my hope & trust that we were to meet again. . . . Of her who is more recently gone I need say the less as you knew her well. . . . I have been blessed with two whose conduct to me has been angelic.

Of Harriet's role in his life, he wrote:

> When I formed my last connection I was considerably advanced in years; & had
> it not been for her strong mind, & for her never failing anxiety to save me from
> every discomfort, I verily believe that in my last years of official life I should
> have broken down. How I have suffered from each of my dreadful losses can be
> known only to myself; but this last blow came upon me when I had no longer
> strength of mind or of body to bear up against it, & the effect has been to throw
> me for the remainder of my life very much into retirement.

Two months after Harriet's death Charles had assured his son that
Wellington had said that 'I may rely upon his being always a friend to
my children to the utmost of his power . . . in reply to a prayer of mine
that if he outlived me he would be as kind to you all as he could.' He
went on to describe his own situation:

> I have had many dreadful nights – quite sleepless ones. . . . For many days I had
> scarcely an hour's sleep in 24 hours, & that sleep was produced by opiates. You
> will not think that with the mind thus praying upon itself I could possibly attend
> to my concerns or indeed to anything; but rely upon it that when I have strength
> & calmness of nerves, my great object will be to perform all the duties of life,
> feeling as I do that by performing them I shall best prepare for death, & for the
> Rest which I hope will follow Death.

He declared that he was 'weaned from the World' and that he had
endured 'as much mental misery as I think I could suffer' and was
'prepared for my own departure'. 'Every hour of my life shows to me
more & more', he wrote in December, 'what a blank is before me till I
go into my grave.'

Others wrote of their feelings at Harriet's death. Wellington's letter to
Lady Shelley has not survived, but she wrote in answer to it from Milan
to assure him

> How well I understand your feelings; no one can replace her! That union of
> frankness and discretion which I so much appreciated, and which made her so
> valuable a friend, gave you – from the experience of many years – a repose in her
> society which no one else can replace.

For herself, Lady Shelley recalled her delight in Harriet's company, and
how much they both loved to talk of the duke together: 'the knowledge
that I shall never see her again, makes a terrible blank in my life!'
Wellington replied

> Alas! our poor friend! I wish that she had gone to meet you, or anything rather
> than to her last home. . . . It is impossible to describe the effect produced by her
> death. It is felt by all. Poor soul! This is the very time which she had settled to
> come here [to Walmer for their autumn visit] . . . But it is impossible not . . . to
> lament her every day, more and more.

Over a year later, in November 1835, he wrote that he still missed her 'more and more every day' and that 'her poor husband . . . will never recover'.

Harriet's sister Caroline wrote to Charles's daughter two days after her death to enquire after her father and assure her that 'I feel for him more than I can express. I well know his devoted attachment to my poor dear lost sister, and can well imagine what must be his state now!' She hurried to Fulbeck to comfort 'my poor Mother who I know must be wretched indeed'. Harriet's body was taken to be buried at her family home, in accordance with the wish she had once expressed in a letter to her mother and now quoted by her brother Henry. Charles seems to have been unaware of this and had planned the funeral at Woodford, but he gave way to her family's wishes all the more readily because Woodford now had unbearable associations for him and he had determined not to live there permanently. He was comforted to some degree by Mrs Fane's and Henry's assurances of their 'very warm affection' and their sense of 'his unremitting kindness and devotion to our dear sister'. Whether these words obliterated Charles's memory of their doubts about the marriage twenty years before is not recorded: he seems rarely if ever to have visited Fulbeck afterwards and when he died in 1850 he was not buried beside Harriet but at Kensal Green.

Charles's life after Harriet's death was a solitary one apart from the time he spent with Wellington, when the duke was able to get away from his continued political duties as leader of the Conservatives in the House of Lords. Charles assured him in 1836 of his sense of 'yr never ceasing kindness to me . . . were it not to see you & to be with you I should pass the remainder of my days alone.' He had no taste for the society he had enjoyed when Harriet was alive: in October 1839 he dined at the Grevilles' in Grosvenor Place but felt a fish out of water among a company he scarcely knew: 'The whole of the dinner I was wishing myself back again with you at Walmer', he told the duke. He felt that he was 'in company with Whig Radicals; I was therefore quite silent all the time I was with them.'

Wellington's affection for Charles, whether for his own sake or out of continued remembrance of Harriet, never wavered. Lady Salisbury wrote in 1835 of his 'good nature and kindness': 'nothing can be more irksome to a man of his active mind than a visit to a solitary broken-hearted man like Mr Arbuthnot who has lost all energy and interest in everything.' The duke was mindful always of Charles's feelings: no company was asked to dinner on the anniversaries of Harriet's birthday, when the two men dined alone. Their solitary evenings were often spent, as Francis Fane, a young subaltern, remembered, in telling stories of their past lives and reminiscing together. In their later years their housekeeper at Walmer remembered how they used to walk together on the ramparts, 'our two dear old gentlemen so happy together'.

Charles was nevertheless thankful, as he wrote to his son in 1838, to have kept a number of 'good & most valuable friends'. His retired way of life 'only takes me from scenes which could amuse me no more; & which if it were possible for me to mix in them, which it wd not be, would only divert my thoughts from what alone ought now to occupy them' – mainly meditation upon religious topics and preparing himself for his own death, whenever it might come. 'I do assure you', he wrote, 'that the greatest consolation I can ever have here below is thus to reflect, & to be aware at every moment of my life that I may suddenly be called away.'

These rather morbid reflections did not prevent Charles from continuing to take an interest in politics and even on occasion to try to resume his former role as a political conciliator and adviser to the leaders of the Conservative party, as it now became known. In particular, he sought to smooth the relationship between Wellington and Peel which was often difficult. He had told Peel in May 1834 at the time of the duke's election as Chancellor of Oxford that the duke 'speaks to me more openly than he does to most persons; and I think that I am rendering him a service, as I am meaning also to render one to you, by letting you know what his thoughts and objects are.' He continued to perform this service in the following years. 'The only way in which I can be of the slightest use', he wrote in January 1839, 'is by doing my best that our two leaders, in the Lords & Commons, should know exactly what is passing in each other's minds . . . but [he added] I don't live much in the World, or mix in general Society, and I may be wrong'.

The continued exclusion of the Conservatives from power, especially after Queen Victoria's accession in 1837 and her close relationship with Melbourne, fostered Charles's habitual pessimism. 'I am sick at heart with this sad state of things', he wrote to Peel late in 1839. 'I had hoped to have seen England herself again before I leave this World; but I have scarcely a ray of hope remaining.' He was distressed at the thought that Victoria might marry Albert, whom he considered to be 'a thoroughgoing Radical', and when he heard that she had proposed to him he remarked that 'We have a haughty little Lady for our sovereign'. In the following January he was pleased that the House of Commons had insisted on reducing the proposed grant to Albert from the civil list as it would be 'a useful lesson to the Queen, & will prove to her that Her own ungovernable will cannot in this country be Her only rule of conduct'. He also opposed the grant of precedence to Albert who 'can never be more than subject [or] rank above those who by their birth

Charles Arbuthnot in old age: S. Gambardello

may come into the possession of the crown'. As long as Victoria remained a partisan of the Whigs, and 'we cannot have Her love, it is well to make Her respect us & know our strength'.

The situation changed in 1841 when Melbourne's government seemed about to fall and the Queen, who under Albert's influence had got over her pique and displeasure with the Conservative leaders, promised that she would 'honestly' give them her confidence. Charles had thrown himself eagerly into his old role during the general election which returned the Conservatives with a strong majority and had busied himself in helping to manage the elections in several constituencies. Charles devoted his efforts to ensuring that the duke should be in the Cabinet as leader of the House of Lords, and when the administration was formed in August he was also in the forefront of discussions about other appointments. His contacts with the royal court were now useful: his son Charles was on duty with his regiment at Windsor and had become a friend of Baroness Lehzen, Victoria's former governess, and through her had become known to and something of a favourite of the Queen. She had twice asked him to dinner. When Peel became Prime Minister she made the young Charles an equerry in waiting. Two months later Peel offered to help him to get into Parliament, but after

Woodford Church in the early nineteenth century

discussion with his father he decided that he would be more useful picking up gossip at court than in the House of Commons.

Charles's pleasure at the return of a Conservative administration and his own part in helping to bring it about lifted his spirits. He noted with approval in October 1842 that there was a growing rapport between Albert and Peel, so that the Queen's former commitment to the Whigs was weakened. Though Wellington's influence over the ministry was less than Charles would have wished, he continued to act as an intermediary to transmit the duke's views. Peel's increasing remoteness from his followers, however, exacted its price in 1845, when the decision to repeal the corn laws on the pretext of the famine in Ireland once again split the Conservatives and led to Peel's downfall, engineered by Disraeli and Lord George Bentinck: the latter's speech against Peel in June 1846 was deplored by Charles as a 'vile and blackguard attack', but he nevertheless blamed Peel for splitting the party: 'I am no protectionist', he wrote, 'but had Sir Rt. been more conciliatory to his supporters, & more confidential towards them, none of the evil would have occurred.'

Peel's defeat, and his death in 1850, ended the short interlude of Conservative government in over four decades of almost unbroken Whig or Liberal supremacy. Charles outlived him by only two months. Towards the end of the decade his health began to become precarious, with symptoms of heart disease and failing appetite. In August 1850 his condition worsened, and on Sunday the 18th Wellington, on returning from the Chapel Royal, found him rapidly weakening. His sons and daughter-in-law were beside him and read prayers to him. Wellington took his hand and 'felt the cold in the ends of his fingers' as the end approached. Charles told the duke that 'it was satisfactory to him to feel that he was going. He was quite quiet, and his appearance as satisfactory as I could imagine that of any man at such a moment.' Shortly afterwards he asked to be left alone except for one of the physicians, and died at about ten minutes past three, 'without struggle, convulsion, or apparent pain, just as a flame or candle would expire from extinction', Wellington wrote. 'His has really been the death of the good and upright man, worn out by disease.' Wellington followed him two years and one month later. The 'most unusual, subtle, and successful essay in triangular friendship' was over.

Envoi

Charles and Harriet Arbuthnot lived at the centre of London society and political life in the nineteen years after Waterloo and their friendship with Wellington was a major feature of that life. From his office in the Treasury and in the House of Commons Charles had an unrivalled vantage point from which to observe and get to know all the inner secrets of politics. During the long administration of Lord Liverpool and more briefly under Wellington he was privy not only to important decisions but more especially to the inner workings of the system of patronage and personal interest on which the political world rested. His boast that for over twelve years he was consulted by the Prime Minister on every appointment in government and in those other fields in which government patronage was dominant was a justified one, while Castlereagh for one declared that Charles's advice was always sought in matters of difficulty. He was above all a conciliator and intermediary in keeping the path of government smooth, whether concerning George IV as Regent and King and his relations with the Cabinet, or between individuals in the government. In particular he became the eyes and ears of Castlereagh and Wellington, and in a real sense the political agent of each, protecting their interests and serving their advantage whenever he could. He was less an originator of policies than a smoother of their paths, and he subordinated his own views and interests to those of others. He identified himself so closely with Wellington in the 1820s that he was considered to have no views of his own. Greville alleged that he 'is weak, but knows everything; his sentiments are the Duke's.' However, while he might appear to have been the duke's mouthpiece, he held firm Tory principles with deep conviction. He believed in the rule of the aristocracy, and rather like Edmund Burke thirty years before, saw himself as a 'man of business' to the great men of rank and position who were fitted to govern but were too lofty to concern themselves with the minor details of affairs. He lacked Burke's intellectual equipment, but he was ambitious in the sense that he valued his good name and wished to be involved in important matters. In 1828 he was deeply hurt when Wellington failed to reward his devoted service with a place in the Cabinet, but he was too modest to consider that he rightfully belonged there because of his talents.

Charles indeed was unfit for the highest offices in politics. He was thoroughly honest but he was not a leader of men, had no great personal presence, and was too apt to hesitate about decisions. He was nervous and fussy about details, and consequently sometimes too dilatory in despatching business. Even in his private affairs he was subject to what he called 'my *confounded* nervousness' and if Harriet was away he was in 'a fuss & turmoil' until her daily letter arrived. As he wrote in June 1825, 'I am nervous about you lest you shd be unwell; I am nervous about poor Caroline; I am nervous about our Duke; perhaps I am nervous about dinners . . . '. When he had to travel to London he fussed about whether to travel by the coach or by the mail and could not decide until the last moment. Wellington wrote that 'tho' a clever man, [he] had an anxious restless mind, always worrying himself when he ought to be acting, and depending upon her for advice, for consolation, for everything.'

In his public career this temperament was a handicap to him. He was accused of forgetfulness over the details of parliamentary management and he complained that he was criticized if he whipped supporters in when it was not necessary, or if he failed to do so and the division was too close. He was not a good speaker, though he often had to hold the fort when senior ministers were not present, and he admitted this defect when accepting Wellington's refusal to put him in the Cabinet on those grounds, though one suspects that it was not the duke's only reason. Despite their close friendship, Wellington realized that Charles was not up to the demands of a senior office, and his lack of rank and family background disqualified him from the more passive and prestigious appointments. Had it not been for his marriage to Harriet, with her more positive and assertive manner, Charles would have been forgotten as a hardworking but on the whole ineffective politician of the second rank.

Charles Greville summed him up:

Arbuthnot's career has been remarkable. He had no shining parts, and never could have been conspicuous in public life, but in a subordinate and unostentatious character he was more largely mixed up with the principal people and events of his time than any other man. . . . Few men ever enjoyed so entirely the intimacy and unreserved confidence of so many statesmen and ministers, and therefore few have been so well acquainted with the details of secret history. . . . [He was] much liked, much trusted, continually consulted and employed, with no enemies and innumerable friends. This was owing to his character, . . . Without brilliant talents, he had a good sound understanding and dispassionate judgement, liberality in his ideas, and no violent prejudices. He was mild, modest, and sincere; he was single-minded, zealous, serviceable, and sympathetic (simpatico), and he was moreover both honourable and discreet. The consequence was that everybody relied upon him and trusted him, and he passed his whole life in an atmosphere of political transactions and secrets.

If Charles was the more cautious and sympathetic of the two, Harriet was by far the more strong-minded. She was devoted to her fussy husband and many a time she had to encourage him and stiffen his resolution in face of difficulties, for example when he was fretting over their pensions after his retirement. She was essentially a political woman. Politics was a lifelong obsession, and her friendships with men were motivated by the access they provided to the political world. There is no doubt that she was attracted to Castlereagh and to Wellington personally, finding in their company both emotional and intellectual stimulation, but the question as to whether she was ever the mistress of either can probably be answered in the negative. Conclusive proof is lacking either way, but her letters to Charles show a constant love and devotion to him, and when she was accused in anonymous letters of being the duke's mistress she and the duke and Charles were able to discuss the allegations calmly without any signs of guilt. Lady Shelley, who was perhaps her most intimate female friend, had no doubt that she was never unfaithful to Charles, and believed that she lacked any powerful sexual feelings. She never had children, and as Charles had sons and daughters by his first marriage Harriet must either have been incapable of childbearing or must have taken care to avoid pregnancy. She built up a loving and trusting relationship with her stepchildren, but whether she had any of the qualities required in a loving mother may be doubted. She confessed on more than one occasion that she was not fond of small children, so she must have lacked the maternal instinct.

Harriet's true *métier* was in the salons of London and in the political world in general. She was intelligent, a good conversationalist, though limited by her obsession with Tory politics, and very down-to-earth. Lady Wharncliffe, who got to know her for the first time in 1833, thought she was 'a clever agreeable person to talk to, a clear good head, & well-informed on many subjects. But [she added] she is certainly neither pleasing nor interesting'. Robert Raikes considered her 'a very clever, agreeable woman, and, from her great intimacy with the Duke, a prominent feature in the Tory party'. It was this sharpness of mind allied to political prejudice that made her seem disagreeable to those who did not share her views. Prince Pückler-Muskau, a visitor from Germany, sat next to her at a magnificent dinner at the Rothschilds in 1827 and found her 'very clever' but 'an *enragée* politician'; he confessed that he must have 'annoyed her excessively; in the first place, I am a great Canningite; in the second I hate politics at dinner'.

Harriet's involvement in politics was at bottom an emotional one, and this is why it was so intense. She had no patience with compromise, hated Whigs, radicals and reformers, and used her considerable influence over Wellington to try to push him into ultra-Conservative policies. Sir Henry Hardinge, who knew her well, thought that she harmed the Tory party by setting the duke against Peel, whom she never liked and often criticized in her journal for what she considered his arrogance and untrustworthiness. In reality Peel's faults as a political leader stemmed more from shyness than arrogance, but Harriet had no time for excuses. She judged men by their external conduct and rushed into conclusions – her heart ruling her head.

Nevertheless, she could be a kind, considerate and thoughtful friend, with a genuine love of quiet domesticity – so long as it did not last too long – and of her home and garden at Woodford, which she came to love for Charles's sake despite its rural seclusion in remote and dreary Northamptonshire. She was genuinely if conventionally religious, and moral to the point of prudishness in her disapproval of improprieties of dress, language and conduct. Here too she was quick to condemn: she had no patience with attempts to excuse or understand. Sir Robert Heron, a Lincolnshire squire who knew her well from her childhood, wrote:

> Dying at 40, she had not survived her beauty: highly accomplished, admirably well-informed, particularly in all that could be learned from the best company, utterly without affectation, her manners were fascinating and her conversation most agreeable. She was highly esteemed by the first Statesmen of the tory party, and as she was naturally pleased with their attentions and society, and encouraged by her husband, with whom she always lived in the most affectionate union in conscious innocence, she rather imprudently despised the malice of public opinion . . . .

To Wellington, Lady Shelley observed, Harriet was what he needed, 'a fireside friend, and one quite without nerves'. She had no reverence for or shyness with the duke, as Lady Shelley had: 'We three together', Lady Shelley wrote, 'formed a perfect union, where no jealousy or littleness of feeling ever intruded to destroy its harmony'. With Charles too, Harriet and the duke formed a triangular relationship of great trust and perfect intimacy. These relationships lay at the heart of Harriet's life and stood at the centre of Tory politics in the 1820s.

Sources

This book is intended for the general reader as well as the academic specialist and so I have deliberately spared the reader the tedium and distraction of detailed references and footnotes. Academic readers will readily recognize the sources of information I have used. For others, a few general remarks may suffice.

The chief sources used throughout the book are the Arbuthnot papers in King's College Library, Aberdeen, a selection from which was published by Professor A. Aspinall as *The Correspondence of Charles Arbuthnot* (Royal Historical Society, 1941: my quotations are from the original MSS); the Fane family papers at Lincoln (County Record Office); and Harriet's journal, published as *The Journal of Mrs Arbuthnot*, edited by F. Bamford and the Duke of Wellington (Macmillan, 1950). I was refused permission to consult the original MS or the collection of the first Duke of Wellington's private correspondence, both kept at Stratfield Saye. A few of the duke's letters to Harriet are printed in *Wellington and his Friends*, edited by the Duke of Wellington for the Roxburghe Club in 1965. Harriet's letters to the duke, which must have been very numerous, were destroyed, as was the duke's habit with his correspondence. His official correspondence is in the Wellington papers at Southampton University.

Manuscripts

The Collingwood, Huskisson, Liverpool, and Peel papers in the British Library.

Printed source material

The Autobiography and Memoirs of Benjamin Robert Haydon 1786–1846, A.P.D. Penrose (ed.), 1927.

Bagot, Josceline, *George Canning and his Friends*, vol. 2, 1909.

Bury, Lady Charlotte, *The Diary of a Lady-in-waiting*, 2 vols, A.F. Steuart (ed.), 1908.

The Correspondence and Diaries of the Rt Hon. John Wilson Croker, vol. 1, L.J. Jennings (ed.), 1884.

The Correspondence of Charlotte Greville, Lady Williams Wynn, R. Leighton (ed.), 1920.

The Correspondence of Lady Burghersh with the Duke of Wellington, Lady Rose Weigall (ed.), 1903.

Despatches, Correspondence, and Memoranda of Arthur, Duke of Wellington, vol. 1, 1819–22, Duke of Wellington (ed.), 1867.

The Diary and Correspondence of Charles Abbot, Lord Colchester, vol. 3, Lord Colchester (ed.), 1861.

The Diary of Frances Lady Shelley, 2 vols, R. Edgcumbe (ed.), 1912–13.

The First Lady Wharncliffe and her Family 1779–1856, vol. 1, Caroline Grosvenor and Lord Stuart of Wortley (eds), 1927.

Gleig, G.R., *Personal Reminiscences of the First Duke of Wellington*, M.E. Gleig (ed.), 1904.

Greville, C.C.F., *A Journal of the Reigns of King George IV and King William IV*, 3 vols, H. Reeve (ed.), 1874.

The Greville Diary, 2 vols, P.W. Wilson (ed.), 1927.

Hansard's Parliamentary Debates.

Heron, Sir Robert, *Notes*, 1851.

Later Correspondence of George III, 5 vols, A. Aspinall (ed.), Cambridge, 1962–70.

Leaves from the Diary of Henry Greville, Viscountess Enfield (ed.), 1883.

The Letter-Journal of George Canning 1793–1795, P. Jupp (ed.), 1991.

The Letters of Harriet Countess Granville 1810–1845, 2 vols, Hon. F. Leveson-Gower (ed.), 1894.

The Letters of King George IV, 3 vols, A. Aspinall (ed.), Cambridge, 1938.

Manuscripts of Earl Bathurst . . . 1665–1834, Historical MSS Commission, 1923.

Manuscripts of J.B. Fortescue Esq . . . 10 vols, Historical MSS Commission, 1892–1927.

Memoirs and Correspondence of Viscount Castlereagh, second Marquess of Londonderry, 12 vols, C.W. Vane (ed.), 1848–53.

Oman, C., *The Gascoyne Heiress: the Life and Diaries of Frances Mary Gascoyne-Cecil 1802–39*, 1968.

Private Correspondence of Lord Granville Leveson-Gower, 2 vols, Castalia, Countess Granville (ed.), 1916.

Raikes, T., *A Portion of the Journal kept by Thomas Raikes . . . 1831 to 1847*, 4 vols, 1856–7.

A Regency Visitor (Prince Pückler-Muskau), E.M. Butler (ed.), 1957.

The Times.

The Torrington Diaries, C.B. Andrews (ed.), 1954.

The Wynne Diaries, 3 vols, A. Fremantle (ed.), Oxford, 1935–40.

Yonge, C.D., *The Life and Administration of Robert Banks, Second Earl of Liverpool*, 3 vols, 1868.

Secondary works

Arbuthnot, Mrs P.S.-M., *Memories of the Arbuthnots of Kincardineshire and Aberdeenshire* (1920) (includes Charles Arbuthnot's fragment of autobiography).

Aspinall, A., *Politics and the Press c.1780–1850* (1949).

Crook, J.M. and Port, M.H., *The History of the King's Works*, vol. VI, 1782–1851.

Gray, D., *Spencer Perceval, the Evangelical Prime Minister* (Manchester, 1963).

Grego, J., *The Reminiscences and Recollections of Captain Gronow*, 2 vols (1890).

Hinde, Wendy, *Castlereagh* (1981).

Hinde, Wendy, *George Canning* (1973).

Hyde, H. Montgomery, *The Strange Death of Lord Castlereagh* (1959).

Jackson-Stops, G., 'Fulbeck Hall', in *Country Life*, 17 February 1972.

Longford, E., *Wellington*, 2 vols (1969, 1972).

Maxwell, Sir H., *Life of Wellington* (1899).

Parker, C.S., *Sir Robert Peel* (1891).

Thompson, N., *Wellington after Waterloo* (1986).

Wilson, J., *A Soldier's Wife: Wellington's Marriage* (1987).

Index

And will your Ladyship ever remain cruel, & insensible to emotions which you alone can excite? –
Oh you flatterer! Every boa knows your devotion for Woods & Forests: therefor don't talk to me of Love, false man! my heart bleeds only for my persecuted friends of the true Church in Ireland. You are the only man in Christendom who is able to emancipate them. Grant me this favor, dearest, most illustrious her and then – perhaps – I could – –